Happy
Returns, Daddy
All my love
Sue
xx

A CHANCE TO LIVE

Action for Dysphasic Adults is a
registered charity which was set up in
1980 to provide information and advice
to dysphasic people and their carers. If
you would like to support their work
by making a donation, or if you would
like further information or advice,
please contact them at:
Canterbury House
1 Royal Street
London SE1 7LN

If you feel that you would like to
support the work of the **National
Hospital for Neurology and
Neurosurgery** please send your
donation to:
The National Hospital Development
    Foundation
The National Hospital for Neurology
    and Neurosurgery
Queen Square
London WC1 3BG

A CHANCE TO LIVE

Marchioness of Tavistock
and
Angela Levin

HEADLINE

First published in 1991
by HEADLINE BOOK PUBLISHING PLC

10 9 8 7 6 5 4 3 2 1

British Library Cataloguing in Publication Data

Tavistock, Henrietta Joan
  A chance to live.
  1. Great Britain. Social life, *1936–*   Biographies
  I. Title   II. Levin, Angela
  941.084092

ISBN 0-7472-0353-9

Typeset in 11/13½pt Times
by Colset Private Limited, Singapore

Printed and bound in Great Britain by
Richard Clay Ltd, Bungay, Suffolk

HEADLINE BOOK PUBLISHING PLC
Headline House
79 Great Titchfield Street
London W1P 7FN

Contents

To Robin

Foreword

by Lady Tavistock

When I was first told that Robin had had a stroke and that he had only a few hours to live, all I could think of was: how can I go on without him? Yet, once I saw him in hospital, unconscious though he was, I believed he would not die. Miraculously he lived and has made a marvellous recovery. There are many reasons why – the prompt action taken when it happened, the incredible medical care, our family and friends who never ceased willing him to live, plus his own courage and determination.

Many people found his story so moving and inspiring that they suggested a book should be written. At first I was reluctant because it has been a very private and emotional period in our lives. Yet it has also been one of the most rewarding, and I realised that it was important to share what we have learnt from the experience. I knew nothing about strokes, but now I know more and have learnt much about coping with someone who has had a stroke and with myself.

I only decided to tell the story because Robin wanted his story to be told. He wanted to give people hope; to make them realise that nothing is impossible. We both felt it was important to be honest and open in the telling of it. Above all we hope that it will help people to understand that someone who cannot communicate in the usual way doesn't necessarily have any difficulty in thinking rationally and clearly. So many people appear to believe that understanding is inextricably linked to communication. This is the big battle that people who have suffered brain damage have to overcome, and having lost the ability to communicate they cannot do it by themselves.

It is for this reason that my share of the royalties will be divided between the redevelopment fund for the National Hospital, Queen Square, and Action for Dysphasic Adults. The National Hospital cares not only for people who have had strokes but for all who have illnesses of the central nervous system. Action for Dysphasic Adults is a registered charity set up to provide information and advice to dysphasic people and their carers. It aims to raise awareness of dysphasia and its consequences, which have been overlooked for too long.

Henrietta Tarnstock

Introduction

by Lord Tavistock

I wanted this book written because I want people to realise that however ill someone is, they should never give up. I was one centimetre from death, but I am now 80 per cent better. I know Henrietta never gave up. I often wonder what would have happened to me if she had.

After my stroke I had incredible difficulty in putting even two words together, but although my language will never be 100 per cent, today my sentences are quite good and my comprehension is total. My chances were, in many ways, the same as everyone's and my speech therapist was on the National Health.

Since my stroke I have met a lot of people who have had some brain damage and are suffering from dysphasia. I have met many like me who know what they want to say, but can't get the words out. I want to prove to people that they shouldn't treat us as idiots. I want people to realise that improvements can take a long time and that they must be patient. I realise that in this respect I am in an enviable position. People have to have time for me.

I want to persuade people not to hide stroke victims away. They should take them out, help them try to speak, try not to let them get depressed, and ignore other people's embarrassment.

I thought the book should be written honestly and I think people will be interested in knowing what I was like, what has happened to me and how I have changed. In the past my life was far too regimented. I worked seven days a week and all hours of the day and night. I couldn't see any way out of it. Perhaps that is partly why I had the stroke. Now I realise that life is wonderful and it means a great deal to me.

I want to be an inspiration to others and help people realise that many of my and my family's problems were and are the same as theirs.

The story of my stroke is an amazing series of coincidences. What has happened to me could happen to anyone.

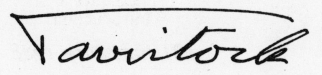

Chapter 1

21 February 1988

Lord Tavistock telephoned security at 5.30 a.m. They were not alarmed. He had got into the habit lately, even on cold winter Sundays, of calling down well before dawn, to ask for a cup of tea before he started work. The butler, Roger Holmes, who would normally bring his tea, was not due in until 7.30 a.m. The 48-year-old heir to the dukedom of Bedford was a tall, handsome man with a firm chin and an aristocratic bearing. A man who took life seriously and worked hard. At the moment the pressure of work was even harder than usual. As well as his substantial business involvements in London, and running Woburn Abbey, one of Britain's premier stately homes, he had taken on the additional responsibility of raising extra money for the Kennedy Memorial Trust. He had set himself the target of raising £1 million, which he was determined to meet. He hadn't looked well for a long time, and had been having severe headaches, but this was no doubt due to the strain of his working too hard.

It was assumed his workload was also making him withdrawn, bad-tempered and difficult to get along with. The atmosphere at Woburn had been tense and heavy for some time.

It was particularly bad that weekend because on the Friday Henrietta, the Marchioness of Tavistock, had been telephoned by her father from his home in Marbella, to say that her mother was seriously ill and had been given forty-eight hours to live. She

1

immediately flew out to Spain with her second son Robbie, leaving her husband at Woburn with their youngest son Jamie, who was recovering from a bout of flu and was not at Summer Fields, his boarding-school.

Lord Tavistock, a highly organised and meticulous man, had planned his day carefully. He decided to take a break from work after breakfast so that he and Jamie could begin training China, his young black labrador, using a blank firing pistol. He would then work until noon when they would have another session with the dog. Lunch would then follow at 1.00 p.m. when they would be joined by his eldest son Andrew, after which Lord Tavistock would drive Jamie back to school, in Oxford.

The first part of the morning went exactly to plan. China's first training session went well. On his way back to his office Lord Tavistock told Jamie to come back for him at noon. Knowing what a stickler his father was for punctuality, Jamie came into the office on the dot of 12.00 p.m. His father was talking on the telephone. He noticed that although usually immaculate, his father had spilt some coffee down himself. It was something that he had never seen happen before.

Suddenly China jumped on to the sofa and started barking wildly. Almost simultaneously, Lord Tavistock dropped the telephone, spilling his cup of coffee all over the floor. He collapsed on to the sofa and began making strange groaning noises. For an instant Jamie thought that something was wrong. But as his father's noises became stranger and more animal-like, Jamie thought he must be expressing his anger at the dog for jumping on to the sofa. His father had seemed under such pressure lately, so distant and unapproachable, that it was really good to see him playing the fool. Jamie burst out laughing. Roger, the butler, heard the laughter and took the opportunity to come into the office to collect the mid-morning coffee tray. He turned the door handle expecting to see a happy family scene, but his smile froze in horror as he saw Lord Tavistock first vomit and then begin to choke.

He initially panicked. What should he do? He quickly came to his senses. His wife was an ardent fan of televised medical programmes and insisted on telling him all about them, including the gory bits, as they got ready for bed. Mostly he hadn't really listened, but this was an emergency and he forced himself to concentrate.

Fortunately his memory cleared quickly. He knew the first action was to stop Lord Tavistock choking and to keep his airways open. He laid him down on the floor in what his wife had described as the recovery position. He put him on his side, then bent his upper leg and arm at hip, knee, shoulder and elbow so that they were at right angles to his body. He pulled the lower arm out backwards. He felt he had got it right. Then he took off Lord Tavistock's shoes and tie and undid his trousers, so that there was nothing to restrict his circulation. He noticed that Lord Tavistock had a trickle of blood from his nose. Hadn't his wife told him that that was one of the signs of a stroke? He was sure it was. Having done that, he telephoned for an ambulance and then called two local doctors, Dr Logan and Dr Muir. Dr Logan was rarely at home at lunchtime on a Sunday and was walking out of the door to play golf as the telephone rang. He listened intently to what he was told and rushed round to the abbey, his clubs still in the back of the car. He was there within ten minutes. He examined Lord Tavistock, who by this time looked ashen grey, gave him an injection and fitted an oxygen mask and a drip. About five minutes later, and much quicker than had been expected, the ambulance arrived. Amazingly enough an empty ambulance was on its way back to base and happened to be passing very near Woburn at the time. Had it had to come from a distance it might have arrived too late.

Jamie felt guilty for having mistaken his father's collapse for a joke, 'But,' he recalled, 'even at that stage I wasn't really worried. I thought he had probably just passed out.'

Lord Tavistock was being put into the ambulance when Andrew rang from his car. He was on his way from his home in Newmarket but was a bit delayed so he wondered if lunch could be postponed until 1.15 p.m.? He was told his father had fainted. Although it had never happened before, he was not unduly worried but just to confirm that everything was all right, telephoned again ten minutes later. This time Roger was consulted about what to say. 'Tell him that his father is quite ill and that the ambulance is taking him to Milton Keynes hospital and that he should go straight there,' he advised.

Andrew put his foot down on the accelerator and sped towards the hospital. Various thoughts rushed through his mind. Should he telephone his mother immediately or wait until more concrete news? Perhaps his father had just fainted after all and it would be wrong to alarm her unnecessarily, particularly when she was already so worried about her mother. On the other hand perhaps it really was serious. He decided he had better warn her just in case. He telephoned Marbella and told her what he knew.

He then rang David Sieff and David Wolfson, both close friends and trustees of the Bedford Estate. With their impeccable medical connections they would be able to give him advice.

Meanwhile at Woburn Abbey, Roger asked security to get hold of Meg Buckenham, Lady Tavistock's personal assistant, and Denis Garrod, the Woburn Abbey administrator. Roger then climbed into the ambulance. He was shivering, partly from nerves and partly from cold. The day could not have been more bleak. He had a nasty feeling in the pit of his stomach that Lord Tavistock might die on the way and in order to protect Jamie from any further distress, persuaded him to follow in the doctor's car. Jamie, who now realised that his father was seriously ill, cried most of the way to the hospital.

As the ambulance sped away, its siren blaring, Roger held the drip and talked gently to the man he had admired for nearly twenty years since he first came to work at Woburn in the catering department when he was sixteen. The journey to the hospital took twenty minutes, but to Roger, it seemed more like twenty hours. The ambulance arrived at 1.20 p.m. By coincidence, and there were many that surrounded Lord Tavistock's stroke, a top anaesthetist, Dr Jeevananthan, happened to be passing by the casualty department when Lord Tavistock was admitted. Dr Jeevananthan was not normally at the hospital at weekends but immediately took control and administered vital sedatives to try to stabilise Lord Tavistock's critically high blood pressure. Roger and Jamie were shown into a tiny waiting-room.

After a while a doctor came in and asked to speak to Lady Tavistock. Roger told him she was in Spain. He looked gently at

Jamie then asked Roger to step out into the corridor. Although Roger's prompt action had certainly saved Lord Tavistock's life at the time, the prognosis was poor. He was unlikely to live for more than six hours. Roger went back to the waiting-room. He broke the news to Jamie, who took it calmly. Roger couldn't stop himself from shaking. Then one of the doctors came to ask Jamie if he would like to see his father for probably the last time. Jamie walked to where his father was lying on a table in the emergency room. 'He looked like someone lying in state,' he said. He was sure his father would die. He was then taken back to the small dark waiting-room. Roger had gone to make some telephone calls and Jamie sat there alone staring at a poster of a spine.

He wondered how long it would be before Andrew arrived, but most of all he thought about his mother. He hoped somehow she would be able to get back from Marbella while his father was still alive.

Andrew arrived at the hospital having driven 'like a maniac'. His right leg had not stopped shaking throughout the journey.

He was taken to see his father, now a dreadful shade of green, in the emergency room. One of the doctors came to speak to him. The doctor explained to Andrew that his father had obviously had a stroke. His blood pressure had been a terrifying 240 over 140 when he arrived, but since the sedatives had been administered and he had been put on a ventilator, it had dropped to 130 over 80, which was still alarming. Neither his pupils nor his limbs were showing any signs of life. Andrew was told that the best place for his father would be the National Hospital in London. He discussed the matter with Charles, Viscount Chelsea, Lord Tavistock's cousin by marriage, who had arrived at the hospital very anxious and keen to help. Lord Chelsea agreed that the National Hospital was the best place and inquiries were made to see if they had a bed. However, medical opinion was that he was unlikely to survive the journey. There was no indication that he would live longer than the original assessment of six hours. Two hours out of the six had already passed and taking into account the lack of facilities in an ambulance, there was a less than fifty: fifty chance that he would make the trip. His father could, of course, stay at the Milton Keynes hospital but, apart from

5

stabilising his condition, there was nothing more they could do. They were not equipped with a brain scanner or any of the other sophisticated equipment needed to save his life.

This was the life-or-death decision facing Andrew. He remembered how his father had been so marvellous to him when he had been involved in a near-fatal car crash in America when he was fifteen. Now was a chance to repay his dedication. He weighed up the pros and cons carefully. If his father stayed put he could only deteriorate. If they could get him to the National Hospital they might be able to save his life. But it was a big risk. How would he feel if his father died in the ambulance? But wasn't he likely to die anyway if he was left at Milton Keynes? Andrew looked at his watch. It was already 2.30 p.m. – another half-hour out of the six had been lost. He took a deep breath and told the doctors he wanted his father taken to London.

It was going to be a race against time. As every minute counted, he asked if the hospital could organise a police escort. He was told one would be waiting as soon as the ambulance reached London. Hopefully the traffic would not be too bad so early on a Sunday afternoon. By the time everything was organised it was 3.00 p.m. before they set off.

Andrew got into the ambulance with his father, two nurses and two doctors, one of whom was Dr Jeevananthan. He had been about to go home, but instead volunteered to accompany Lord Tavistock and handle the crucial and expert task of monitoring the ventilator and administering the right amount of sedation to keep his body functions as stable as possible. Jamie followed in a car with Alex Hay, managing director of Woburn Golf and Country Club, and his wife Ann.

Although speed was of the essence, the medical team was so concerned that if the ambulance travelled too fast, it could cause his condition to deteriorate further, that it was decided that they would not travel at more than 40 m.p.h. even on the motorway. As the ambulance set off into the gathering darkness of a cold and gloomy winter's evening, Andrew gently held his father's hand. He talked quietly to him, telling him where they were and that he shouldn't worry. But the confidence he tried to instil in his unconscious father hardly masked his own despair. His father used to drive down the motorway to London so many times each week. Would this journey be his last? Sunday 21 February, exactly one month after his father's forty-eighth birthday, would be one he would never forget.

The police escort joined them right on cue as they reached London and they sped through the streets with Jamie right behind. They had not gone far, however, when another police car arrived on the scene and stopped the car that Jamie was in. Andrew watched anxiously through the window of the ambulance as it sped away. He hoped there was nothing very wrong. He didn't feel he could cope with any extra anxieties.

It turned out later that the police had thought Jamie's car was ambulance chasing, and when they discovered the true situation, let the car continue its journey. When the ambulance arrived, Lord Tavistock was immediately whisked upstairs to the Harris Intensive Care Unit on the first floor.

Meanwhile news of his sudden illness was spreading fast. Meg had telephoned everyone she thought should hear the news directly and by the time Lord Tavistock reached the hospital, Lord Francis Russell, Lord Tavistock's half-brother, was already there.

Andrew stayed with his father while the doctors plugged him into several machines. He was then told that several friends had arrived and were waiting downstairs. They included Lynda Berry, Jeni and David Sieff, Sir David (now Lord) and Lady Wolfson, Charles Price, the American ambassador, and his wife Carol, and Countess Bunny Esterhazy.

Countess Esterhazy remembers thinking: There are far too many people here. It is not a cocktail party. Someone is dying. She stayed none the less. 'I was determined to be there when Henrietta arrived. I knew that although she would be very shaken, she's very tough, a great planner, and wouldn't fall to pieces.'

Andrew watched the doctors trying to make his father as comfortable and peaceful as possible. 'Then,' he said, 'I thought I had better go and speak to the friends waiting downstairs. But I didn't feel like talking very much and quickly went back upstairs to the ward again. Somehow I couldn't stay there very long either and came back down again and saw Susan Wolfson and Jeni Sieff who were both obviously very upset. I went up to Jeni and hugged her and she said, "Don't worry, it'll be all right." I just burst into tears. Until that moment there had been so much to decide and do that I'd just tried to cope with everything and hadn't had a chance to think. I don't usually show much emotion, but crying was a great relief.'

Lord Chelsea arrived and went up to see Lord Tavistock. 'He looked just like a corpse,' he said. 'I decided not to stay but to go to the family's London home in Clarendon Place and deal with any telephone calls.'

Roger had meanwhile taken Andrew's car and driven himself back to Woburn. He quickly packed a bag of things Lord Tavistock might need and was driven to the National Hospital by Roy Harrison, the chauffeur. At the hospital he felt overwhelmed with despair. He also decided to leave and go to Clarendon Place. He was sure Lord Tavistock would die and knew he wouldn't be able to control his feelings when he saw Lady Tavistock. A similar thought was in everyone's minds. Would she get back in time to see her husband before he died?

*   *   *

In Marbella, the day had begun sadly for Henrietta Tavistock and would nearly end in tragedy. She had spent the morning with her father discussing how he would be if his wife died, little realising that she herself would be in a similar position a few hours later. She remembers the day vividly.

My parents' housekeeper was off that day and I'd just gone into the kitchen to prepare some lunch when the telephone rang. It was Andrew calling from his car. He said, 'I've just been told that Daddy fainted and they've taken him to Milton Keynes hospital.' It didn't occur to me for one moment that he'd simply fainted. My instincts immediately told me that it was very serious. I said, 'He wouldn't faint. He's either had a heart attack or a stroke.' Andrew told me he was going straight to the hospital. I immediately rang Woburn. I was again told that he had fainted and I shouldn't worry. I felt annoyed. I prefer to make up my own mind if

I'm going to worry. I just wanted them to give me the facts. Then I rang James Bevan, our family GP in London, and asked him to telephone Milton Keynes hospital as they would obviously give a doctor more information. Dr Bevan is very rarely available at lunchtime on Sunday. But like everyone else on that day he was there; it was as if everyone had it in their diary that on Sunday 21 February they were going to be needed very badly by the Tavistock family.

I rang Robin's father Ian, the Duke of Bedford, in Méribel, where he was skiing. His wife Nicole answered the telephone. I told her I didn't know how seriously ill Robin was, but I felt she should tell Ian. She told me she couldn't get hold of him for the rest of the day, because he was skiing. I said, 'That's ridiculous. All you have to do is notify someone at every ski lift and they'd find him.' I rang a friend in Marbella and asked her to get Robbie and me seats on a flight to London. She phoned back to say that all the flights were booked. I think both Robbie and my father thought I was over-reacting by making all these telephone calls and immediately trying to come home, but my instincts told me otherwise. I'm very good in a crisis, I go on thinking and planning until everything is done and arranged and then I go to pieces.

Although I admit I exaggerate trivia, I never exaggerate when things are really important. Within an hour my instincts were proved correct. Andrew telephoned me again, this time from Milton Keynes hospital, and told me that Robin had had a stroke. I asked to speak to one of the doctors. He was brutally frank and he told me my husband had just six hours to live and that I might not see him alive again. Then Meg, my PA, rang and I asked her to get me a private plane to fly me home, as we couldn't get seats on any plane to London.

She tried Gerald Ronson, but he was away and all his pilots had done their quota of flying. She tried Karim, the Aga Khan, my husband's cousin by marriage, but his plane wasn't around either. I called Charles Chelsea, Robin's cousin who had been best man at our wedding. He has a flying company and I asked his advice on how I could get back from Marbella.

He too is very rarely at home on a Sunday, but was also at the right place at the right time and immediately left his lunch party and rushed to Milton Keynes hospital to be with Andrew, who is his godson. It was only after all these telephone calls that I suddenly realised the best person to help would be Lord King, chairman of British Airways. His wife Isabel answered the telephone when I called and said Meg had just called and her husband was on the other line making arrangements for us to fly back.

I also asked Andrew to telephone Robin's best friend Chuck Downer, who went to school and university with him and whom he has always loved more than anyone else in the world. They are more like brothers than friends. He lives in Boston. At first Andrew said he would call him when he had more news, but I told him to ring right away because Chuck might then be able to catch the last plane that evening. When Andrew called he had seventy minutes to get to the airport and get on the plane.

I knew I had to go to Robin, but I was also desperately worried if I would ever see Mummy again. I went into her bedroom, sat on the bed, took her hand and said, 'You always said the most important thing in life is timing. At the moment your timing is terrible as I'm going to have to go because Robin is seriously ill. Daddy will stay with you and I'll be back when I can.' Somehow, as ill as she was, she must have understood as she lived for another fourteen months.

My parents' house was about an hour's drive from the airport, but a friend Rex Holton, who lives in Woburn village and with whom we jointly own the Woburn garage, was staying in Marbella at the time. I rang to tell him about Robin and within a few minutes he was at the house to take Robbie and me to the airport.

There had been so many calls to make and things to do that it wasn't until I sat in the car and on our way to Malaga airport that the reality of what had happened began to sink in. That hour's journey from our house to the airport was the worst journey of my life. I was sure that Robin was going to die. I remember thinking: I must move out of Woburn within a week because it will pass to Andrew on Robin's death and if I stay Andrew will find it very hard to ask me to leave later. Stately homes like Woburn are not women's houses.

Robbie too felt devastated by the news. 'Sometimes my mother exaggerates quite a bit but on this occasion I was sure she wasn't. I felt as if my whole world had been pulled out from underneath me. I tried not to think about if my father died, but I couldn't help myself.

'I felt that if he died I would be on my own. When I was growing up, he'd always been the one to keep me on the right tracks whether I liked it or not. I suddenly felt I had to grow up and take more responsibility and for the first time really appreciated what he has done for me. I also felt very emotional about leaving my grandmother. I wondered whether it would be the last time I would see her too.'

On the journey to the airport both mother and son tried to be as brave as they could for each other. But they both cried a lot. 'Of my three sons,' said Lady Tavistock, 'Robbie is the one I have the most communication difficulties with and he with me. I was pleased he was the one with me because he often finds me unapproachable and then he saw me at my most vulnerable.'

Robbie agreed. 'My mother and I have had an up-and-down relationship and tend to argue a lot. From the minute we left the house to go to the airport, until we landed at Gatwick, we got very close. I mainly cried on the way to the airport and she comforted me. She mainly cried on the plane and I tried to comfort her. I stopped thinking so much about my father and concentrated on how my mother was feeling and what she must be going through.'

Henrietta
The British Airtours cabin crew had obviously been told about us because they put us right up at the front so we didn't have to look at anybody else and treated us with deliberate care. Throughout the two-and-a-half-hour flight we

didn't know whether Robin was dead or alive. I had an awful aching feeling in my stomach. I thought back to the time when Robin flew out to the States to see Andrew after his car accident and didn't know throughout that flight whether our son was alive or dead. We landed at Gatwick and British Airways had a car at the foot of the plane which bypassed the airport building completely and took us to the perimeter of the airport where we were told another car was waiting for us.

As the British Airways car stopped and we got out, I saw David Sieff and David Wolfson get out of their car. Without saying a word they walked towards us and gave me and then Robbie a hug. I thought: He's dead, that's why they're hugging me; and I got into the car without saying anything. I decided I had to hear them say the words. I plucked up my courage, took Robbie's hand, squeezed it very tightly, and asked, 'Is he still alive?'

They both said, 'Oh yes and holding on well.' I'm afraid I then lost my temper and said, 'The minute you saw me you should have said, "He's alive." We didn't know how he was all the time we were in the air. Never ever do that to me again.' I'm afraid it was very ungracious of me.

They then rang the National Hospital from the car telephone to say that they'd picked us up and we were on our way. The hospital reported that there was no change in his condition. They had diagnosed a brain haemorrhage and that there was tremendous pressure on his brain and the surgeon would be at the hospital waiting to talk to me. I heard that many of our friends had already rushed to the hospital, including Charles and Carol Price who by chance had been staying with the Kings when I telephoned.

When Lady Tavistock and Robbie arrived they both rushed up the stairs to the Harris Intensive Care Unit on the first floor. Robbie walked into the room where his father was lying but walked out almost immediately. 'I couldn't deal with all the tubes, machines, nurses and doctors,' he said. 'The shock was too great. I started to cry, but didn't want to cry in that room so I came out. I saw my uncle Francis there who felt the same as I did and we went for a walk together round and round the square in front of the hospital.'

Lady Tavistock then walked in to see her husband on her own. Her reaction was quite different.

Although there were tubes and electronic equipment everywhere and Robin was on a ventilator, he looked just as if he was sleeping peacefully. All the strain had gone from his face and he looked years younger. His colour was fine, he looked relaxed and in no pain. Sitting at his head was a young nurse called Julie whose face I shall always remember. It was totally serene. I immediately trusted her and suddenly felt totally safe. I held Robin's hand and touched his face. I'd never seen anyone look that peaceful and from that moment on I didn't doubt that he would live.

Chapter 2

Childhood and Adolescence

There is no duty so much under-rated as the duty of being happy.
Robert Louis Stevenson

Henrietta

I feel Robin's stroke was an act of God to stop him working so hard and to learn how to enjoy his life. But it was as if a whole infrastructure had been planned to make sure he didn't die. I've often thought about the day when he so nearly died. One of the strangest things I've realised is that although his stroke happened on a Sunday, the worst day of the week for finding anyone you needed, on that particular Sunday, everyone was where he needed to be, at exactly the right moment, to help save Robin's life. Even the timing of his stroke was extraordinary. If it had happened a couple of hours later, he would have been taking Jamie back to school. If it had happened during the previous or following night, I would have been in Marbella and no one would have been there to hear him or save him.

As it was, Roger walked into Robin's office the moment he had his stroke and was able to administer vital first aid. An empty ambulance was passing close by and rushed him to Milton Keynes hospital. There was a skilled anaesthetist at the hospital who stabilised his condition and looked after him on the long life-or-death journey to London. There was a bed available at the National Hospital. Lord King was at the end of the telephone to get Robbie and me home and many others helped in so many ways.

It was a pattern that was to continue throughout Robin's recovery. The individuals crucial to his return to health – his surgeon Alan Crockard, his nurse Tania Lorking and his speech therapist Eirian Jones – all materialised just when they were needed.

I feel that my whole life has existed to prepare me for and help me cope with Robin's illness.

So many things that I have done, have, since his stroke, taken on a new meaning and significance. I've thought so often: My goodness, if that hadn't happened to me, I'd never have been able to deal with this for Robin. So many things I've been through in my life have given me the insight, the experience, or the ability not to mishandle situations that occurred during his stroke. It's a preparation that I feel goes right back to my childhood and upbringing. Even my parents spoiling me enabled me to spoil Robin.

* * *

I was born in London on Tuesday 5 March 1940, in a nursing home in Bentinck Street, London W1. I was a Caesarean baby because my mother was over forty, five feet one inch tall, and had never had a baby before. She was asked what day she wanted to have me and she decided to have me on a Tuesday, because of the poem that says, 'Tuesday's child is full of grace'. She thought that to be 'full of grace' was most important. I have always liked Tuesdays. My coming-out party was on a Tuesday, Robin and I got married on a Tuesday and by chance Andrew was born on a Tuesday.

Mummy had several operations before she got pregnant. She told me she was so determined that nothing should go wrong when she was pregnant with me that she asked the doctor how he could be absolutely sure that everything would be all right. He told her to stay in bed for four months, which she did.

It was very sad. She really wanted to have lots of children, a big, happy family which she herself hadn't had, but in the end there was only me. She had a little boy called Edward two years later, but he died when he was only six months old.

We lived at 69 Avenue Road, St John's Wood, London, which my parents built just before the war. It was a wonderful house.

My mother had an unhappy childhood. Her own mother was not very maternal. She sent her to boarding-school in Broadstairs when she was only three, and only had her home in the summer holidays. My mother didn't talk about her very much. But she did talk about school which she liked. She always wanted to act, and became a well-known actress. Even when she was at school she produced and acted in plays. I'm really sad that I never saw her on stage. I've got some of her films – but they were made during the early days of the cinema and they are not very good technically. By all accounts she was wonderful on stage and looked incredibly beautiful. She called herself Joan Barry after Sir James Barrie, the author of *Peter Pan*, whom she greatly admired. Her real name was Ina Florence Marshman Bell. Much later my parents called their house in Spain 'Casa Ina', but Mummy was always called Joan. She went on the stage when she was sixteen and left home at about the same time. She was in a play called *Springtime for Henry*, which Nigs, the Marquess of Willingdon, took my father to see. Mummy joined them afterwards for dinner at the Embassy Club. She and Daddy danced together all evening and he fell madly in love with her. Nigs later became my godfather.

My father, Henry Frederic Tiarks, was meanwhile very unhappily married to Millicent, the daughter of the Marquess of Headfort. He had married at twenty-eight in St Margaret's, Westminster, there were two thousand guests. I remember him telling me that he ran over a black cat on their way from the wedding reception to Dover where they were catching a boat to go on their honeymoon. He took it as a sign that things would not go well. He was right. He hadn't realised that his wife didn't really like men. Her girlfriend even joined them on their honeymoon. It must have been terrible for him. When he told me about it, I asked him how he could have married her and not known. He explained how life was very correct then and you would never have lived with anyone before marriage. They remained married for about ten years and had a son called Christopher, who died of meningitis when he was two. Apparently he died in my grandfather's house in Somerset. My father's wife and her girlfriend arrived just before Christopher died and left soon afterwards, leaving Daddy alone with his son.

Daddy then put the body of his son in the back seat of his car and drove alone with him from Somerset to Chislehurst where all the Tiarks family are buried.

I remember him saying to me once that I probably think of him as someone incapable of showing emotion, but that he felt a large part of his emotion died on that journey.

My father was thirty-eight when he met and fell in love with my mother. As he was a Catholic, he tried to get an annulment, but his first wife said if he got an annulment, she would never give him a civil divorce. In the end he had to be satisfied with a civil divorce. It made him desperately anti-Catholic.

Emmy, my father's mother, was German and apparently a lovely woman. I can't remember much about her as she died when I was three. His father was Frank Cyril Tiarks, a brilliant merchant banker who was a director of the Bank of England and, amongst other things, a director of the Anglo-Iranian oil company. I remember he used to go to Persia, as Iran was then called, by ship every year, sailing through the Red Sea. He was a wonderful man whom I absolutely adored. I used to have such lovely times with him as a child. He originally lived in a large Gothic house called Foxbury in Chislehurst where he had two polo fields. When he retired he went to live in the village of Loxton near Axbridge in Somerset. The house had been built as a hunting-lodge. My grandfather, whom I called Gump, had two packs of hounds there, the Mendip Foxhounds and the Mendip Harriers.

I remember once during my holidays, when I was five or six, going for a walk with him across the hill. I was picking primroses and putting them into a basket. We came across a sheep having twins. I'd never seen any animal born before and when the mother sheep had given birth to the second one my

18

grandfather said, 'I don't think she'll be able to bring up two.' He picked up one lamb and put it in my basket with the primroses, and we took it down to the farmer who owned the sheep.

For the rest of those holidays I was able to give the lamb a bottle. I'm sure Gump had taken it so I could have a pet lamb. When Robin and I later bought our country house at Chevington and the children were small, I told Robin it would be wonderful for them to have a lamb. I suppose it was really that I longed to have one again myself.

My grandfather died when I was thirteen. I think he was probably as difficult a father-in-law to my mother as my father-in-law has been to me. My mother was never happy in his company and therefore I have always felt guilty about how much I loved him. I still feel very close to him and think of him often. Even now when I really can't cope and everything is getting on top of me, I drive to Loxton and sit on his tombstone and talk to him and sort it all out. I went when Robin was ill. It's sad Robin never knew him. They would have liked each other very much.

When I was two Mummy had Edward. He had mild Down's Syndrome and not long after his birth caught gastro-enteritis. During the war there were no antibiotics and tragically he died when he was six months old.

I remember the day he died very clearly although I was so young. Nothing had been explained to me, but I knew that something was very wrong. I remember walking into a room and seeing people silhouetted against the light and thinking they looked like cut-outs. They were all looking out of the window because they were crying. From that time I was always very wary of Mummy's feelings. Sometimes I'd walk into a room and she'd hug me and I'd realise she was crying.

Robin and I first met when we were two, but I don't remember it at all. Apparently we'd both been invited to the same children's party. Robin's mother was ill and rang my mother to ask if we could take him. She was thirteen years older than Robin's father, and about the same age as my mother. The war was on and we were temporarily living in Stanmore where

Daddy was stationed in the RAF. The party was at Claridge's, and we picked Robin up on the way. Mummy said that as she walked with one of us on each hand she thought: How funny, when they both grow up, they could get married.

We went to the same kindergarten in Ordnance Hill, St John's Wood. My nanny and I used to walk past Robin's house and pick him up on our way to school. From the age of four we also went to the same dancing class with Miss Ballantyne. Apparently Robin wouldn't dance with anyone if he couldn't dance with me, but I can't remember that. My first real memory of him is after his mother died and his father had remarried. They were living in Acacia Road which was about three minutes' walk from our house and they used to come to tea. Once, just before they arrived, Mummy said to me, 'You've got to be very nice to Robin because he's a very sad little boy because his mother has died.' I remember him vividly. He had knobbly knees and was as thin as a stick. His hair had been badly cut and he was wearing an awful pair of shapeless, thick, grey shorts. I thought he looked such a sad little person and he wouldn't be any fun.

Although from the outside my parents didn't seem compatible, they absolutely adored each other. I wasn't, however, brought up in a family environment. There was no one around from Mummy's family and my father never seemed close to his, partly because they did not seem to like my mother. In the thirties, although it was fashionable for a duke to marry an actress, it wasn't approved of by my father's rather Germanic family. I think they must have thought actresses and ladies of the street were one and the same. They apparently made her feel very unhappy and unwelcome.

My father had a wonderful life as a young man. He used to play polo after the City every night. It took him twelve minutes by car from the City to Foxbury near Chislehurst in Kent. He's never had a driving licence because in the twenties if you could afford a car, you had one. He told me of one wonderful Rolls-Royce that having done 100,000 miles, ended its days pulling the mowers on the polo ground.

He loved hunting, spear-fishing and skiing. He's been an

enthusiastic photographer since he was seven and even now he's ninety, he carries several cameras and videos around with him. He speaks French, Spanish and German fluently and even taught himself Russian when he had TB and was invalided out of the RAF in 1942.

I've never really worked out which characteristics I've inherited from each parent, which I suppose is odd as I spend an enormous amount of time planning the mating of my horses purely on their parents' characteristics.

I think I'm probably more like my father. Daddy and I have a very strange relationship. We argue all the time. He now lives in Marbella and we only ever see each other in three-day, four-day, or six-day periods. Because we are similar we sometimes say very hurtful things to each other but seem to bear no grudge afterwards. You can only do that with someone who is very like yourself because you both know you can recover from the hurt. I could never have done the same with my mother.

I have enjoyed being an only child, but I probably wasn't the right child for my mother. When I think of her I think of gentleness and everything pretty and feminine. She liked everything to be beautifully done. She couldn't bear imperfection. I, on the other hand, was much more of a tomboy and quite independent. Like most little girls I was sent to ballet and tap-dancing classes and I remember the teacher saying to my mother that it was a waste of her money sending me to ballet classes, because it would be easier to teach a hippo to dance. If you had asked me my dream when I was eight or nine, I would have told you I wanted a female horse so she could have foals, and a horse-box to drive her about in so I could take her with me everywhere.

That was the sum total of my ambition. I didn't want to get married and have a big family myself. I thought then and still do that being an only child is wonderful.

I always preferred looking after horses to riding them. I started riding when I was about three, but was never a courageous rider. Daddy used to like to ride with me on Sunday mornings in Windsor Park and was disappointed that I wasn't very brave. He adored hunting, but that's the only thing to do with the country he ever really loved. He's a city person. He finds the country too dull.

My mother didn't like the country much either. I, on the other hand, never liked living in London and have always been much happier in the country.

Another thing Daddy and I have in common is our untidiness. I've always been messy and I remember my mother constantly going round after both of us tidying things up or throwing them away. Daddy was always keeping newspapers and you needed a whole house for his collection of photographs.

My father is very intelligent, very scientific and interested in everything, particularly astronomy. He discovered a star from the Eton Observatory, which he founded. It didn't matter what I asked him when I was a child, he would always explain it to me or, if he didn't know the answer, we'd look it up in the encyclopaedia. He retired from banking in 1968 and even at ninety, he's still very active and prefers to do everything at a run. He's remained curious about things and about what makes people tick. He's always been very gregarious and really loves parties.

My mother was quieter and tended to enjoy things in retrospect.

I, on the other hand, have always lived in the now and if something is wonderful, I enjoy every single second of it as it is happening. So much so that I tend to wipe nasty things out of my mind. I remember saying to Robin once, after we'd had a row, 'If we ever get divorced I'm not going to be able to sit and tell a lawyer all the terrible things you do because once you've done something nice it wipes the rest away.' Mummy, however, wasn't like that. She remembered all the bad things as well as all the good things that anybody had ever done.

The longest conversations Mummy and I had were when she was in the bath. The only outdoor interest she had was her garden. She had lilies planted underneath the terrace so the lily heads came to the level of the terrace and in the summer the smell was unbelievable. It looked wonderful too, because all you saw were the lily heads and not the rather ugly long stems.

Our garden had a big lawn with a big herbaceous border. There was a deep shrubbery at the back of the garden. I used to make little chapels with altars amongst the shrubs, putting night-lights and flowers in small glass holders.

Although I have always believed in God, I'm not really anything. I'm not very good about organised religion and think there are good teachings in all religions. For me religion is more a way of life. I'm more spiritual than religious. I do believe in an after-life. I think we probably come back over and over again, until we have been taught what life is all about and learned all its lessons. I feel sure I've been here before and will probably come back again.

I have never been confirmed. My father and I discussed it and I said I couldn't be confirmed until I didn't believe that Joseph was Jesus's father. I felt Jesus could be the Son of God, but I felt God didn't impregnate Jesus's mother. I believed Joseph did. I felt having such a belief prevented me from being confirmed. Had I been told I couldn't have got married in church without being confirmed, I suppose I would have been. Mummy and Daddy would have hated it if Robin and I had got married in a register office. I would have too.

The church I really liked as a child was the one I used to go to with my grandfather. It was a tiny Saxon church and very simple. The most comfortable thing about Christianity for me is that Jesus was born in a stable. It's cathedrals I can't cope with. I think such lavish buildings are man trying to show God how wonderful he is. Cathedrals are elevating to visit, but I would never be able to communicate with God in such surroundings. In fact right up to the time Robin had his stroke, I usually felt embarrassed and uncomfortable in a church. But when I went to St Clement Danes church during his operation, I felt for the first time in my life that I had an open line to God and that He was with me.

When I was small I had several nannies, but when I was six a wonderful nanny arrived who stayed with me until I was fourteen. Her name was May Alberta Ponder. We used to travel quite a bit and whenever Daddy filled out Nanny's immigration form he always asked her at the top of his voice, 'What is your name, Nanny dear?' She used to go bright red.

She left to marry Daddy's chauffeur, which didn't turn out well. Nobody knew it, but he was already married. She had two daughters and a son by him and was pregnant with her fourth child when the police came to arrest him for bigamy and he was sent to prison. She had the new baby adopted, her son, who suffered severely from diabetes, died when he was about seventeen, but her daughters are now grown up. She is now married to a really nice man. We write to each other and I see her every two or three years.

Nanny was tiny, like my mother, and I absolutely adored her. She was a great opera fan and whenever an opera was on the radio in the evening, she would get me out of bed and let me listen. I'm very grateful to her for giving me my love of opera.

Nanny was not the old-fashioned, very respectful type of nanny, and had quite a quick temper. My mother was probably a bit jealous of our relationship and I think resented having a nanny. They used to have awful arguments. Even though I was quite young, the animosity between them made me very aware that you have to be very careful about the feelings of people you love.

I sometimes forgot myself when it involved my grandfather. I remember being taken by Mummy and Daddy to Portofino in 1949 where we'd been lent a lovely villa on top of a hill. As we walked up the hill my mother said, 'Isn't this wonderful?' And I replied, 'I would so much prefer to be with Gump at Loxton.' I realised once I'd said it how ungrateful it sounded.

We had a wonderful cook called Mrs Fairbrother, who was with us for over twenty years until she retired. Her two daughters used to help in the house. We also had a parlourmaid called Anne and a marvellous man called Ernest Squires who used to come three mornings a week to clean the silver, press Daddy's clothes and polish his shoes. I've never known anyone who could clean shoes like him. I loved to sit and watch him. Squires was very keen on racing and as I grew up we spent a lot of time talking about horses. I'm sure he contributed to my love of racing. When my parents emigrated to Spain, he came to work for Robin and me three days a week. He also worked for Lord Olivier and Dame Peggy Ashcroft.

I was very lucky growing up in beautiful surroundings and having really nice people looking after us.

After nursery school I went to a day school called Miss Lambert's in Queens Gardens W2 for a couple of years, but when I was seven Mummy decided to get a governess and educate me at home. There were two reasons. One was that every winter I seemed to catch one cold after another and she thought it was ridiculous that she got me better from one and then as soon as I went back to school I caught another. She was worried I'd never learn anything. The other reason was that Daddy travelled a lot. He loved Mummy to go with him but she hated going for long unless she could take me. As a result my education became patchy. So from the age of seven until I was about eleven, I did all my lessons at home with one or two friends who lived nearby. I had two French governesses. The first one was called Mme Montadent Smith, who only taught French. The other was Mlle Salles. She was wonderful and made learning really fun. It sounds weird, but I read every single Shakespeare play in French. She took me to museums and opened my eyes to the fact that you can never be bored because there is so much to learn and read and do. She taught me to sew; she did beautiful embroidery. And she was animal-mad. I loved animals too and had a rabbit, a tortoise, a dog, a cat, goldfish and birds. It was paradise. Mummy filled the house with lots of children, because she was worried that I would be lonely. But I never was.

I was quite a stubborn child, but not very naughty.

Mummy liked me to look pretty and I had an incredible number of clothes. After the war, clothes in England were rationed and rather austere and when Mummy went to America she brought me back trunkfuls of clothes. Compared to many of my friends, I was probably rather overdressed or at least too prettily dressed. I don't think it helped me make friends. I wore little white gloves, white socks and hair ribbons

25

until I was twelve. Nanny would put my naturally straight hair into curlers every night.

When I was eleven I went back to Miss Lambert's school. I think Mummy worried that I wouldn't be like other children and that I might get lonely. I still have friends from school, including Susan Davies who is now Susan Wolfson. I used to arrive at school in different clothes every day. Nanny laid out my clothes for me every morning. Although the school was only ten minutes' walk away, until I was thirteen Nanny walked there with me and would be standing outside with my dog to fetch me when school ended. I never ever went anywhere on my own. Even if I went to tea with a friend, Nanny would take me and if she didn't stay, come back and fetch me later.

I'm sure Mummy never thought of the effect such over-protection could have on me. She just thought I was very precious and had to be taken care of. My girlfriends who knew me then have told me they thought I was poisonous. I would have hated me too.

I've noticed throughout my life that people who don't really know me have often misinterpreted me. It used to make me sad, but as I've grown older I have realised that it only matters what people I care about think of me. I find it very irritating that no matter what I do, I'm always referred to as 'Henrietta Tiarks, daughter of millionaire banker Henry Tiarks, former Deb of the Year and daughter-in-law of the Duke of Bedford'. None of which has anything to do with what I've accomplished myself. Although it sounds cynical, Robin's having had a stroke has helped my reputation, for many people have perhaps realised that I'm not quite as bad as they thought. I know people believed I changed during Robin's illness. But in reality I do not think I have changed much at all.

When I was thirteen and a half I changed schools and went to Dixon & Wolfe, Tutors in Victoria Street. The teaching was excellent and I eventually got six O-levels and a couple of A-levels.

My parents sold our home in Avenue Road when I was ten. We bought a really wonderful second- and third-floor flat in Hyde Park Gardens which was being converted by the architect

Donald Campbell. The conversion took about two years and in the meantime we rented a house, 25 Radnor Place. I was thirteen when we moved into Hyde Park Gardens.

I was totally unaware of fashion until I was fourteen. The first time I remember ever being conscious of feeling I was looking good was when I wore a grey pleated skirt, a belted yellow jersey, stockings instead of socks, and brown shoes, and went to Swinley Forest golf club for lunch with Daddy. I remember walking round the golf course thinking how terribly grown-up I was.

I was blissfully happy until I was fifteen. I never questioned what my parents told me. If they told me Mrs Jones was nice and Mrs White was nasty, then that is how it was. It never occurred to me not to ask my mother what I should wear. But at fifteen I became negative and difficult and began to do and say the opposite of everything my parents told me. One of the nasty habits I developed as an only child was eavesdropping. I used to hear my mother and father saying, 'Now, if we say this, she's bound to say that. So as we want her to do this, if we do this, this and this, she'll probably do it.'

I thought how odd they were because actually what they thought I'd say and how they thought I'd behave wasn't right at all. Eavesdropping made it terribly easy for me to be absolutely impossible. But there was also a sadness because I realised for the first time that they didn't seem to understand me at all. From that time I was never the daughter my mother should have had. And by the time I could have been, we were sadly not really able to communicate. Mummy gradually withdrew into herself for the last ten years of her life. It so often happens that by the time one has grown up and got the perspective right, it is too late. That is one of the reasons I am so glad that I had Andrew and Robbie when I was young. I've been able to grow up with them.

Chapter 3

Romantic Times

If there were no clouds, we should not enjoy the sun.

Rev John Ray

Henrietta

After school in London my parents sent me to finishing school in Paris and following that I spent six months in Madrid learning Spanish. Mummy felt it was vital to speak languages. She only spoke English and felt at a great disadvantage. I am so grateful to her.

Robin and I saw a lot of each other, especially in the school holidays. He used to spend a lot of time in Cadogan Square with Primrose Cadogan, his stepmother's sister, and her children including Charles Chelsea and we all used to go out together. Although I wasn't allowed to go out with boys then, I was always allowed to go out with Robin. Mummy never thought of Robin as a boy, he was always just Robin. One evening when I was thirteen several of us went to the theatre and at the end of the evening Robin said to me, 'We're all going to Woburn tomorrow. Do you want to come?' I said, 'Yes,' but when I woke up the next morning I decided I didn't want to go. I told my mother and she said, 'Don't be so silly, of course you want to go. It's the most beautiful house and you can wear your new pink tweed suit from Jaeger.' I went.

Primrose Cadogan took us in her car and I remember sitting in the back seat with Robin and her spaniel. Robin and I were both stroking the dog and kept on, accidentally on purpose, touching each other's hands. When Robin was young he used to have very cold hands with red knuckles, but when he grew up they developed into lovely, aristocratic, distinguished hands which Robbie and Jamie have inherited.

He was very shy as he took me round Woburn. When we'd been everywhere he stood in front of the fireplace in the Wood Library and said, 'I hope you like the house.' I had actually been thinking how horrid it must be to live in a house that big. But as I didn't want to be rude, I just smiled.

He then said, 'Well, I'm glad you liked it, because this will one day be your home.' I immediately thought: I'll never ever live here. It didn't occur to me that I would ever marry him.

I remember clearly the first time Robin kissed me. It was in 1956 during the Suez Crisis. I was at school in Paris but had come home with appendicitis. I went into hospital to have my appendix out and while I was recuperating went to Woburn for the weekend. After dinner we went for a drive in the park and listened to the news. Then Robin stopped the car and kissed me. I know the exact spot even today.

I became quite difficult when I was fifteen, but by the time I was seventeen I began to feel a bit of a misfit and was quite unhappy. Looking back I think the years from 1957 to 1968 were the most difficult part of my life. Although I was initially terribly excited about coming out I quickly grew tired of all the fuss and it has become the part of my life that I could well have done without.

It all began when, just before I came out, Anthony Armstrong-Jones, as Lord Snowdon then was, took a photograph of me. The *Daily Express* published it in a competition which asked 'Is this the most beautiful girl in Britain?' and invited mothers to send in photographs of their daughters. The media then began to call me 'Deb of the Year' and I was photographed everywhere.

Coming out, of course, meant being presented to the Queen. I was presented by my aunt, Lady Diana Tiarks, at the same time as her daughter, my cousin Tania. She presented me as my father had been divorced and in those days divorced people could not go to court. In fact it wasn't until the mid-fifties that divorced people were allowed into the Royal Enclosure at Ascot. For my presentation I wore a mid-blue dress, a shocking pink taffeta coat and a hat covered in lilac flowers.

Tania and I shared a really beautiful dance for six hundred people at Claridge's. Robin of course was there. Mummy wouldn't let me sit next to him at dinner. He sat next to Tania. I was cross. Other friends who were there included the Maharaja and Maharanee of Jaipur, Barbara Goalen, Mrs Duncan Sandys, Charles Clore, Patricia Rawlings and Tessa Kennedy.

My coming-out dress came from Pierre Balmain and cost £500 which in 1957 was a lot of money. I've still got it. It's pink satin and the whole of it is embroidered with flowers that have little tiny diamonds to catch the light. It's beautiful. The waist is seventeen and a half inches. My waist is now twenty-nine inches! I was never slim but I always had a small waist. After my dance, it was a party and a ball every night and sometimes two or three on the same night.

My mother and father really did spoil me. I had so many pretty evening and cocktail dresses from designers like Balmain, Balenciaga and Dior. It was incredible. My parents were, however, not very pleased with my behaviour during the season. I had a boyfriend who was the son of the Cuban ambassador. He was very good-looking but very jealous. He didn't want me to dance with anyone else and came with me to every single party and would only let me dance with him.

The idea of me meeting lots of new people didn't work at all. Looking back I think I felt very insecure at that time. I didn't know who I was or what I felt and just being with one person was easier to cope with. I felt very valuable at home, but very valueless in the outside world.

After the Cuban ambassador's son I went out with someone who was twenty-five. I thought he was the most incredible man on earth. He asked me how long I was going to remain a twig on my parents' tree. I was mortified, but it began to make me think. His remark seemed to switch on a light in my head. I became totally negative to anything my parents suggested, which must have been very hard for them because they still thought of me as their little girl. I felt that I had become an adult, but that I didn't have my own thing to do and didn't know where I was going. Although I wasn't very ambitious, I did know that I didn't want to lead a life that just involved going to parties and that I wanted to live in the country and do something useful. Inside myself I felt very lost. At one point I wanted to be an actress and was offered the lead in the film *The World of Suzy Wong*. But in the end I decided against it. I'm much too self-conscious to be an actress and probably have no talent anyway.

I was, however, always very happy with horses. I remember once when I was riding across Hyde Park, I realised that I needed something at Harrods. I rode up to the entrance and the commissionaire held my horse, while I went inside and bought what I needed. Then I rode home again.

I came out in April 1957 and that September I went to a junior college in America called Briarcliffe. I had passed into Radcliffe, which is the female part of Harvard, but Mummy felt the college was too big, so she sent me to Briarcliffe instead. This was the same year that Robin went to Harvard.

Robin and I started going out together. We became closer and closer and in 1958, when we were both eighteen, he asked my father if he could marry me. My father said that he thought we were too young and that Robin ought to discuss it with his father first.

Robin's father refused permission. At the time I was young and spoilt and wanted my own way and thought both fathers were quite unreasonable. But in fact they were absolutely right. If Andrew had come to me at eighteen to say that he wanted to get married, I would have been very upset. I think that had Robin and I got married at eighteen, we were so young that we would not have remained together.

Once Robin and I had been turned down by our parents, we drifted apart for the next two years. Looking back I can see it was the best thing that could have happened because it totally changed the balance of our relationship. When we were eighteen, Robin loved me very much. I loved him too but I was in command. When our relationship began again, it was totally on his terms and he has been in command for the rest of our lives.

After we split up I went to New York and worked part-time for the Ford Agency doing photographic modelling. Because I have a slightly Asiatic angle to my eyes, they thought I had unusual looks and it wasn't that hard to get work.

I was lucky enough to be photographed by Richard Avedon, who I think is one of the greatest photographers in the world. It was the first time I had earned money of my own, but I didn't work hard. My taste of freedom made me feel I had to break away from my parents' influence although I was still too unformed to know what I really wanted to do.

It was while I was living in America that I fell in love with a man a lot older than myself who had a profound effect on me. He was someone who made one feel happy just by being with him. I saw the effect he had on others and how people loved and respected him. He made me aware of what was important in life. I quickly grew up, developed my own set of values and learned that one had to be true to oneself. Because of that relationship and the effect it had on me, I think I became a far better wife.

Robin was studying at Harvard then and we saw each other occasionally. He knew I had fallen in love and it hurt him very much. I have always felt sad about the pain I caused him then, but I think in the long run it strengthened our marriage.

When the relationship was over, I came back to London. My parents and I were invited to a party given by Drue Heinz. She and her husband Jack, chairman of the famous food company, were friends of both my parents and Robin's father and stepmother. Drue was very fond of Robin too and when he was at Harvard, he used to spend weekends at her house in New York.

She used to give the most wonderful party every summer and in 1960 I arrived before Robin. I hadn't seen him for several months but when I saw him walk in – even though it was the one and only time in his life that he looked awful: he had a crew cut and was wearing a dinner jacket and cowboy boots – I was struck by the knowledge that I had made the most terrible mistake and that he was the person I really loved. I felt awful. I wanted the floor to open up so either the person I was dancing with disappeared, or I disappeared.

Robin neither looked at me nor spoke to me. He did, however, dance a lot with my mother, which was maddening for me and very astute of him. I hardly slept at all that night. The following morning I got up very early and went to his mews house behind Belgrave Square and rang the door-bell. He opened the door. I said, 'Can I come in?' He looked at me coldly and said, 'All right.' We went inside and I said, 'I've really made the most terrible mistake. I love you very much and I'm desperately sorry I've hurt you. Please can we try again?'

He was very distant and said, 'You'll have to prove that you are worth my love.' That phrase changed the whole balance of our relationship. Because of the sort of person I am, if I'd married someone who put me on a pedestal and kept telling me how wonderful I was, I'm sure I would have behaved like a monster. Once I get the bit between my teeth I can be so determined to do something that, even when I know it's wrong, I don't know how to stop. I can be so strong-willed that I even frighten myself.

Robin took control at that moment and has had it ever since. His control is what I love most about him. It makes me feel totally safe. I don't want to be in control of myself. Whenever I am anywhere and know Robin is coming, I make sure there is nothing around that will irritate him. I tidy up and make sure the newspapers are folded. I would never give him an unpeeled tomato in a salad because he thinks it's slovenly. Nor can you just empty an ashtray, you have to take a damp cloth and wipe it out. He has always hated people parking in driveways in front of the house and although it has often irritated my friends when I wouldn't let them park outside Woburn or our country house at Chevington, I didn't see the point of letting them do something that would annoy Robin. The discipline makes me feel safe.

When Robin said, 'You will have to prove that you are worth my love,' I knew he meant it and since then that is what I have been trying to prove. In fact it's only since his stroke, that for the first time in my life I have felt useful and needed. Of course I couldn't have done it all without the children and friends, but when Robin was so ill, I think I helped his recovery.

When we were both twenty we went back to my parents and told them we were getting engaged. I had agreed to marry Robin on one condition – that I never would have to live at Woburn. He had promised me that I wouldn't have to as long as I had a son within two or three years of being married. He'd worked out that as his father was only twenty-two years older than he was, it would be natural for Woburn to miss him out and pass straight on to our son. In retrospect it was quite wrong of me to make him give such a promise.

We had planned to get engaged on 8 September 1960, my father's birthday, but Ian married his third wife, Nicole Milinaire, who had been a television director in France, on 7 September, so we got engaged the day they got married.

At that time if you were under twenty-one and wanted to put an engagement announcement in *The Times*, both parents had to sign a letter of authorisation. My father did mine, but when Robin's father signed his, he said to Robin that it was the saddest thing he'd ever had to do for him.

I asked him why he was against our marrying and he said he thought I had had a very interesting life, that I was very intelligent and that I would be incredibly bored married to his son. I don't believe that was the real reason. I think it was because he thought I was independent, bossy, domineering and would make his son miserable. I don't mind him feeling that way. I don't think I'd want one of my children to marry me. I would think I'd been too spoilt and had so much that I would only think about amusing myself, would easily be bored and wouldn't make a very good wife.

My parents had come round to the fact that I was marrying Robin. They had of course always liked him and now felt very relieved that I was getting married, because between eighteen and twenty I had become quite difficult to live with. I think they thought it would be a good idea if I settled down with responsibilities of my own.

Our wedding was planned for 21 June 1961. Robin was at Harvard during the nine months of our engagement, although I visited him quite often and he came back to London in the holidays. He said the most useful thing I could do during those months was to learn to cook, and he gave me a list of the things he liked best, which included soufflés, pancakes and treacle tart. I went to the Cordon Bleu School of Cookery and learned to make the food on his list.

I had a fixed idea about the church I wanted to get married in. I loved driving around London at night, especially if I had a problem I wanted to sort out. I would look at the churches as I drove by and imagine which one I would get married in and I decided on St Clement Danes. I didn't realise at the time how terribly difficult I was making life for everyone. After the war the church was reconsecrated as the Air Force chapel and wasn't used for weddings. Luckily for me Daddy was in the Air Force during the war and so was able to arrange it. It was a curious coincidence that St Clement Danes was near the National Hospital and helped me through the long hours when Robin had his operation.

As the time drew nearer and nearer to our wedding day I began to get cold feet. I wondered if I really loved Robin or if we were getting married because everybody had originally been against us and told us that it wouldn't work.

On the wedding day itself, I thought it would be madness to get married. I reluctantly put on my beautiful dress by Nina Ricci. There were four grown-up bridesmaids and four little ones who were dressed in white with turquoise blue sashes. Mummy wore a beautiful oyster silk brocade suit with brown and black flowers and looked wonderful. Nicole had a shocking pink silk chiffon dress and coat by Balmain. The coat was a shade yellower than the dress. Apparently, a girl in the workroom had burnt the original coat when she was pressing it. They had ordered some more material and made another coat, without checking that it was an exact match.

Once I was dressed, I even more reluctantly got into the open-topped Rolls-Royce that was taking Daddy and me to the church. We had hardly driven any distance at all when I turned to my father and asked if he loved me.

He said, 'What a silly question, of course I love you.'

So I said, 'If you do, prove it today by telling the driver to go anywhere but to the church.'

He replied, 'You can't do that, it's too late, you've got to go through with it. But if you're unhappy, it can always end.'

I didn't know it then but Robin had had something far worse to cope with. My parents had a dinner party at home the night before the wedding and when it was over, Robin went back to spend the night at his father's house.

His father said he had to tell him something that would probably make him rethink about marrying me the next day. He then asked Robin if he realised that my mother had had a Down's Syndrome child that had not survived and that the condition could be hereditary?

Robin said he was quite sure that if there was any danger of it being hereditary my father would have told him.

Robin never mentioned this to me until I was six months pregnant with Andrew. We were in Boston at the time and had arranged to spend the weekend with Ian and Nicole in New York. I flew from Boston with Nicole, and Robin and Ian drove. During the flight Nicole told me how worried she was about my father-in-law because he was sleeping so badly. Naturally I asked why and she told me it was because he was so worried that I would give birth to a Down's Syndrome child like my mother had. I was horrified. Like any young mother expecting her first child I was frightened about what could go wrong and at the time you couldn't test for Down's Syndrome.

I told Robin when he arrived and he recounted what had happened between himself and his father the night before our wedding. I felt very humble and realised yet again what a very principled person he was.

The reception at Claridge's was lovely, but my mood didn't really change. I wondered what on earth I was doing. Robin and I were going to go to Paris three days after the wedding and until then were going to stay at Claridge's. To do things absolutely properly, we left the reception as if we were going away. My going-away outfit, an off-white bouclé coat was also by Nina Ricci. I also wore a large off-white hat with a chocolate-coloured ribbon. When we drove off, I told Robin I wanted to go back home to Hyde Park Gardens. He naturally asked, 'Whatever for?' I said, 'Because the whole thing's been a terrible mistake.'

He took me back and I sat outside my parents' home in the car for ages until Robin lost patience and asked me to make up my mind what I wanted to do. I felt completely panic-stricken, but told him I wanted to go home. He drove off and I went inside. No one was back from the wedding. The flat was empty.

I sat on my bed feeling completely directionless. Then about an hour later I rang Robin at Claridge's and asked him to come and fetch me. He told me that if I wanted to come back I could take a taxi. I did. Nicole had put a small decorated tree in our room with little parcels tied on to it. It was a lovely thing to do. It felt like Christmas. There were things like nail scissors, scent and a pot of *foie gras* for Robin. We had a delicious dinner in our room and then sat and watched our wedding on the television news.

The next morning I felt terribly embarrassed that we had both obviously slept in the same bed and when the waiter came in with our breakfast, I hid in the bathroom.

I was, however, still feeling very odd. I rang Ian and Nicole who lived just across the street and asked them to join us for breakfast. They were over in less than a minute. I think they imagined that there'd been some disaster. When they left I still couldn't stay with Robin, so I went to René who was *the* hairdresser at the time. He had been at the wedding and looked at me absolutely nonplussed when I turned up.

Then I asked one of my greatest friends, Bunny Esterhazy, to join Robin and me for lunch and afterwards the three of us went shopping and on to the cinema. I felt ill at ease.

Two days later we set off for Paris. My parents had given us a car as a wedding present, a midnight-blue Facel-Vega Facellia and we drove round the châteaux of the Loire and had a really wonderful time.

I think we've always had our best holidays driving through France together. We were away for two weeks and when we returned my parents gave a dinner party at home for us. Ian, Nicole and Nicole's children came too and we all watched the film of the wedding.

As I was walking out of the front door in my wedding dress looking terribly pale, Nicole said loudly, 'Henrietta, how did you manage to look so pure and virginal?' I thought my mother would explode.

The next day we left London. We were going to New York on the *Queen Mary*. As Robin had to complete his final year at Harvard, we were going to leave our luggage there so that it would be ready to take to Boston in September. We would then fly to Montego Bay in Jamaica to spend the rest of the summer in my parents' home at Round Hill.

Despite the fact that Robin and I had had a lovely time in France, I panicked again and as we were about to board the boat train, I said to my mother, 'I'm not going. I'm staying here.' My poor mother was beside herself. She came with us on the train and smoked all the way to Southampton. I had never seen her smoke before. She was acutely embarrassed that her child was behaving so badly. Robin didn't take the slightest notice of me and once I realised that I couldn't manipulate him, I calmed down and was fine.

In fact he got the upper hand soon afterwards. We walked into the lovely stateroom on the *Queen Mary* which had been reserved for us and I noticed there were two beds. I said to Robin, 'I thought you asked for a stateroom with a double bed.' He said he had and rang for the steward. When he arrived Robin said, 'My wife would like a double bed.' I have never felt more embarrassed. The steward replied, 'Very well, m'lord,' and left. For the entire five-day crossing if I ever caught sight of him in one of the long corridors, I hid rather than face him.

We stayed in Jamaica for three months, but it wasn't a very happy time. For the first three weeks every few days one of us booked a seat on a plane back to England. When you marry someone you've been a child with, it's terribly easy for you both to be childishly irritating to each other. Whereas it's very hard to be childish with someone you've only met as an adult. You'd feel foolish.

My poodle Bambi came out to be with us. He was quite old and the vet thought that although he would have to do six months' quarantine if we brought him back to England with us, it was better to take him to America for our year away than leave him behind, as he might have pined and died.

Bambi had really never liked Robin before, but when we went to the airport to fetch him and took him out of his crate, he took no notice of me at all but made the most incredible fuss of Robin who was absolutely enchanted.

I became pregnant almost immediately, but no sooner had the doctor confirmed the pregnancy than I threatened to miscarry. Even though we were very young, we decided there was no reason not to have a baby. The doctor said I should stay in bed and on no account have any relations with my husband. When I told Robin this he said, 'Didn't you tell him this was my honeymoon?'

Tessa and Bryan Harris arrived about two weeks later to stay with us. I had to spend some time in bed, but we played cards and laughed a lot. I was being very sick and everything except new potatoes boiled with mint made me feel queasy. Robin and Bryan went out to the reef most days to get lobster, but just the smell of them cooking it made me feel sick.

The summer finally came to a close and we flew to New York to collect our luggage and move into our one-and-a-half bedroomed flat in Marlborough Street in Boston. Robin went back to Harvard. It was the first time in my life I'd had to cope on my own. I had a cleaning lady twice a week, but the rest of the time I made the bed, cleaned the flat and cooked. Robin was at classes all day long. I was pregnant, feeling sick a lot of the time and knew almost no one in Boston. I kept thinking: Thank goodness I'm pregnant because I'll be able to go home to London to have the baby. All I wanted to do was run away. I felt like a fish out of water.

I remember the first time I cooked dinner. I started really early and had a beautifully cooked dinner ready at 4.00 p.m., which was pretty pointless as we weren't going to be eating until 7.30 p.m. I went out and bought everything again. That first dinner went wonderfully. I made *oeufs en cocotte*, roast Cornish game hens, *petits pois à la française* and sautéd potatoes, followed by chocolate éclairs.

It was two or three days later that the trouble started. I had cooked trout with almonds, but the trout wasn't cooked enough and the butter was burnt and when I put it in front of Robin he just looked at it and said, 'I suggest you do this again.' I told him there wasn't any more fish. He looked at his watch and said, 'The supermarket's open until nine.' I was absolutely furious, but it was the best thing he could have done. I got into the car, went to the supermarket, bought some more fish and cooked it again. I suppose I needn't have done it, but I did. It was another turning-point for us.

It was very lucky that we were not in England for the first year of our marriage, because there was no one to run home to. If I'd gone back crying to Mummy and Daddy saying things like 'Do you know he made me cook dinner three times last night?' they would have said, 'How can he treat you like this?' and we would probably have been divorced within a year. Instead I had to learn to cope. No one in this world has ever been able to make me do the things Robin can make me do. This is partly because I had a subconscious understanding of myself – that the only hope I had was to put myself in a double bridle and let Robin have control.

It was also because I felt guilty about having hurt Robin when we were younger and the only way I could prove to him that I really was worthy of him, was to let him always be in charge.

We had good times too. Robin used to bring lots of friends home, particularly Chuck Downer, and I would cook dinner for us all. But overall it was a directionless time for me. I was having a baby, but that was all I was accomplishing.

Looking back, I think our nine months in Boston is probably the reason why we have such a long and strong relationship. It was there that we became a pair. There were no outside pressures and we could lead our own life. And at the end of it, we had our own child.

It was while we were in Boston that I realised for the first time that I was going to have problems with Robin and Mummy. She came out to stay with us for a week and during the entire time Robin neither shaved nor bathed and treated me appallingly. Mummy kept saying, 'Isn't Henrietta a wonderful cook?' and he would say, 'I don't think so.' He was awful. But when I came back from taking her to the airport for her flight home, Robin had bathed and shaved. It was the first manifestation of his saying, 'She's mine and I can do as I like.'

We came back to London for Christmas and stayed with my parents. I had by then decided to have the baby in America, but Mummy persuaded Robin that I shouldn't be in the flat when the baby was born and that we ought to go and stay in an hotel. Two weeks before the baby was due Mummy arrived in Boston and we all moved into the Somerset hotel. Robin surprised me by saying he had to go to New York the following day for a meeting. I said, 'You can't go, I'm going to have the baby tomorrow.' He said, 'Don't be so silly, it's not due for days.' And off he went. Mummy and I took Bambi for a long walk by the Charles River and later went down to the hotel restaurant for dinner. Suddenly I had a pain as though someone had stuck a knife through me and not long after, felt the same thing again. Now I've had three children I know I am not aware of going through the first stage of labour, I seem to go straight into the second stage.

We rang the doctor at the hospital and I tried to contact Robin. He had given me a number that he would ring every two hours, just in case. I rang the number and he'd rung only an hour before, so it would be another hour before he rang again. We took a taxi to the hospital. Mummy was very agitated on the journey and I found her desperately embarrassing. She kept saying to the taxi driver, 'You don't know how dreadful it is to see your child in pain.' By the time we got to the hospital at 10.00 p.m. I couldn't walk so they put me in a wheelchair. We had to fill out lots of forms with my name, Robin's name, our religion, etc. Then they asked my mother, 'What colour is the father?' My mother hesitated and then said, 'He has red hair.'

It soon became obvious that they were thinking about Duke Ellington and Count Basie so thought Marquess of Tavistock could have been black. Robin meanwhile chartered a small plane and arrived early the next morning.

The saddest thing is that I have no recollection of having Andrew at all. As well as giving me a spinal injection, they gave me something called Scopolamine which made me forget everything about the birth. Andrew was born at 2.00 a.m. on 30 March 1962. He was two weeks premature and was born nine months and five days after our marriage.

Chapter 4

Robin and the Russell Family

If you can only give your son one gift let it be enthusiasm.
                                                        Bruce Barton

Robin Russell was born at the Ritz on 21 January 1940. It was a place that befitted his family position, but not his family circumstances. Robin's father, Lord Howland, now the thirteenth Duke of Bedford, incurred the disapproval of both his father and grandfather by marrying Robin's mother and had been abruptly disinherited.

Robin's mother, Clare Hollway née Bridgman, was considered quite an unsuitable match for the young marquess. There was the matter of age. He was twenty-two, she was thirty-five. She had also been married before and already had a son.

Lord Howland, who at birth had been registered as John, but christened Ian, had been living on a rather modest £1,000 annual allowance. Whilst this might have been ample for someone of more modest means, Ian felt it hardly reflected his status as heir to one of the largest estates in the country. The amount barely covered his social engagements. There was a constant stream of flowers and presents to be sent to hostesses who entertained him in a style he ironically was not accustomed to at home. His father, the twelfth duke, kept a very tight rein on the family's purse. It certainly wasn't going to be enough to cover the demands of a wife and child.

Lord Howland found himself in such a desperate situation that he even resorted to trying to work for a living. He joined a firm of estate agents and started at the bottom as a rent collector. But he had never been brought up with the idea that he would have to earn his own living and the exercise hardly came naturally to him. Luckily Clare's first husband continued to pay her an allowance.

There was certainly no comfort or consolation from Ian's mother, Louisa Whitwell. She had not been a loving mother, and Ian was brought up by a nanny and merely presented to his parents from time to time for inspection. By the time Ian married, his parents were legally separated and his mother subsequently faded completely out of his life.

All in all the newly weds just about managed until their child was on the way and then drastic measures were required. Ian wrote a bitter, desperate letter to his father, but his father remained resolute. He then appealed to his grandfather, Herbrand, the eleventh duke. Months passed. His desperation increased. At the last moment, his grandfather relented and said he would accept all the expenses connected with the birth. Clare grasped at this straw and declared that she would have their first child at the Ritz Hotel and nowhere else. And so it was.

Soon after the birth she became ill, the earliest beginnings of what was to lead to a permanent breakdown of her health. It was during one of Robin's mother's bouts of sickness that Robin met Henrietta Tiarks. They were both two, although Robin was six weeks older. From that time onwards they were never to be apart for very long.

Robin has vague recollections of the little Henrietta. 'It is a little hazy, but I sort of remember her at two. Even now her features have not changed much. What she looked like then, she still looks like now. She just has a few lines, but not many. I think she still looks unbelievable today.'

The young lord was an unhappy child and his mother hardly caring. She used to hit his leg with a stick when he didn't walk up the stairs correctly, and when she was particularly cross with him she locked him in a cupboard under the stairs.

She would not cut his hair short but kept it in a pageboy style. Many people thought he was a little girl.

'My mother was a poor mother and very unmaternal,' said Robin. 'There was a lot of tension in the family and I felt my mother and father didn't get on. My mother also had a very bad temper which affected me.'

Henrietta

She looks a formidable woman in her pictures. She was tall and thin and used to hold court to a string of admirers. She apparently led a tempestuous life. I remember much later in our lives when we were at a dinner party in Jamaica with Ian and Nicole, our hostess asked why Robin had been called Robin as it did not appear to be a Russell family name. His father replied that Robin's mother had chosen to give him the name of one of her lovers. Robin was very upset.

Soon after Robin was born, the family circumstances improved. Ian's grandfather, the eleventh duke, arranged for the trustees to pay him an allowance of £2,000 a year. This compares with an allowance of £15,000 a year the duke had given Ian's father when he married. Ian was nevertheless very relieved.

The relief, however, was short-lived. The duke died in 1940, the same year the allowance was set up, and while the complicated tax situation was sorted out, the money was stopped. Ian was desperate. The war was raging and he tried to volunteer but was found medically unfit for military service. The regimental adjutant of the Coldstream Guards was sent the following comment.

'His unfitness is due to a congenitally poor physique and an extremely low standard of resistance to infections and to a general lack of stamina.'

Ian, Clare and baby Robin lived mainly on credit until, in desperation, Ian turned to Lord Beaverbrook, whom he had met at several social engagements. Max Beaverbrook gave him a job as a reporter on the *Daily Express*. It proved a lifeline, he loved the work and there was money coming in at last.

When Robin was four, his brother Rudolph was born and the family circumstances took another dive. After the birth Clare's health deteriorated further. She became infected by a series of boils and abscesses in her ears. It was before the days of penicillin and they made her feel increasingly depressed. She resorted to taking sleeping-pills and pain-killers, but her general condition did not improve. She became so poorly that Ian gave up his job on the *Daily Express* to look after her. He could not then afford servants. Her dependency on pills increased and a year after Rudolph's birth she

47

killed herself by taking an overdose of sodium amytal. An open verdict was recorded.

No one told the five-year-old Robin the truth about what had happened to his mother. 'My father told me she'd gone away on a big ship and I waited for her to come back. When she didn't, I thought she'd gone away because of something I'd done. I blamed myself and kept thinking: What did I do? What didn't I do? I think it has hung over me subconsciously for much of my life.

'As a young boy I was very introverted and didn't have many friends. I never even had a birthday party. I used to wonder why other children had birthday parties and I didn't. Fortunately I was quite resilient and thought: That's what my life will be like. Don't complain. Just get on with it.

'I was terribly lacking in confidence, perhaps because my father didn't give me any. He didn't know what to do with me or what to say to me. I'm afraid he's still the same today. He has great difficulty in having a conversation with me that lasts longer than a few minutes.

'I became aware of him having a couple of girlfriends and then about eighteen months later he remarried. His new wife was Lydia Yarde-Buller. I liked her a lot and she made me feel at home. I also had a stepbrother and sister, Gavin and Lorna, but I don't feel she differentiated between us.' Lydia's first husband had been Captain Ian de Hoghton Lyle who was killed in the war.

'Robin was a shy child who had a girl's hair-style and wore a girl's locket when I first met him,' said Lydia, Duchess of Bedford. 'Even as a small boy he had the Russell walk which is rather like someone treading on eggs. His father has it too. I loved him immediately and never felt I was a stepmother. He always had a very good character.'

The couple married on 12 February 1947 and soon afterwards the family came to tea at the Tiarkses'. Henrietta and Robin were both six. The differences between the two children were very marked.

Robin never had anyone to love when he was very small. I, on the other hand, had an idyllic childhood and never ever wondered if I was loved. Every child thinks sometimes about his parents: If they love me, why do they do this to me? But some of the things that happened to Robin were quite cruel. He used to stand in the driveway at boarding-school on Sunday waiting to be collected, and watching all the other boys leave, but no one ever coming for him. My whole upbringing, on the other hand, was one of total trust. I could trust my mother, my father, my nanny, my grandfather. Nobody that I really loved ever let me down.

It was the exact opposite for Robin, who I think grew up trusting nobody. I don't think Lydia ever made any difference between her children and Robin. I think she was wonderful to him, but she wasn't his real mother.

Once you have trusted, it's easier to continue to trust. If my instinct tells me I can trust people, then I do. I think this helped when Robin had his stroke, because if I'd been like him and not been able to trust anybody, things might have worked out very differently. It is only since Robin has had his stroke that for the first time in his life he knows that many people love him.

When Robin was seven or eight he went to live in South Africa where his father bought a 200-acre apricot farm in the Drakenstein Mountains about forty miles from Cape Town. There he designed and built a house called 'Waterfall'. 'I've always felt my father-in-law should have been an architect,' said Henrietta, 'he is never happier than when he is on a construction project.'

Robin's father's relationship with his own father had deteriorated to such an extent that all communication ceased. 'The only thing I had in common with my father,' Ian says, 'is that we both broke with our fathers.'

Robin was sent to boarding-school in South Africa and then to Le Rosey in Switzerland. 'Until I went to Harvard, I used to change countries and schools all the time,' he said. 'It was very unsettling.'

Lydia had three sisters, Lady Ebury, Joan, who became Princess Aly Khan and is now Lady Camerose and Primrose, Lady Cadogan, and Robin used to spend time with them during the holidays. Although he is not related by blood he feels Joan's sons Karim and Amyn Aga Khan and Primrose's son Charles Chelsea are his cousins.

Robin's half-brother Francis was born in 1950 while they were in South Africa. Robin was already ten and at boarding-school.

Henrietta
Although I don't think they were terribly close due to the difference in their ages, Robin has always done everything he could to help Francis and Francis has always come to him for advice on business matters. Francis was very upset when Robin was ill and came constantly to the hospital. Robin's stroke has made them much closer.

Although Lydia and Ian divorced in 1957 she has still stayed in touch. When I saw her with Robin at the National Hospital after his stroke, you would never have imagined that he wasn't her child. She's never demanded anything from him. The relationship she has with him is on his terms.

The family lived in South Africa until Ian's father, the twelfth duke, died in a shooting incident on 9 October 1952.

Ian was playing golf in South Africa, when he heard the news. The twelfth duke had gone out early in the morning to shoot hawks and cormorants and when he did not return for lunch the estate people started looking for him. When he had not returned by the next morning a full-scale search by police, Royal Marines and Commandos was organised. His body was found in some undergrowth very near the house. He had died instantaneously from a gunshot wound in the head. The verdict was accidental death. His death caused chaos in the estate. If he had lived until the end of the year, various financial provisions he had made would have met the necessary legal requirements and escaped death duty. As it was, death duties of nearly £5 million would have to be met, plus £1.5 million of death duties still outstanding from the estate of the eleventh duke.

Ian and Lydia and the children returned from South Africa but it was too complicated to live in England from the tax point of view and Ian bought a house on St Brelade's Bay in Jersey, which was a tax-free zone. Robin was sent to Le Rosey where he met his lifelong friend Chuck Downer.

'Chuck Downer was the first person I felt relaxed with,' he said. 'Apart from Henrietta I hadn't dared relax with anybody.'

'We hit it off straightaway,' remembered Chuck, now a merchant banker living in Boston. 'I came from a close loving family and adored my parents who were loving, outgoing and emotionally demonstrative. I am that way too. I hug people, male or female. Robin was drawn to that. I think he was already damaged by his childhood. A mother's love was missing at a crucial time in his life. He was very close to Lydia and whatever nurturing he got was from her, but I think it was too little and too late. He never had that warm feeling that someone really cared for him.

'However, we always have had fun together. Although I have known him for so many years, he has never shown me the dark side of his personality. I have never seen him in a depression or a dark mood. He is always up when we are together.'

After a couple of years, Robin changed schools again and he and Chuck temporarily lost touch with each other. Robin, however, continued to keep in touch with Henrietta.

Robin remembers himself as a teenager being 'terribly shy and lacking in confidence. I thought Henrietta was very beautiful and we got on well together. In her presence I had no complexes or at least very few. When I wasn't with her I was like a recluse. Or very nearly. Often when I was in London, I would ring her up and in a casual way ask her out. I always used to say, "Don't worry if you are busy, but I was wondering if you were free tonight, because I'd love to go to the cinema."

'Sometimes she wasn't and I used to feel so upset and cross. It really affected me, but I never told her. She was very important to me then.'

Henrietta was by now going through her difficult teenage stage.

Henrietta

I remember asking Robin what his ambitions were and he said, 'The only thing I want to be is a very good duke.' I thought it was a weird and pathetic thing to say, but I now realise it wasn't pathetic at all. It's like being a good minor king because you hold a certain position in the community and there are a lot of people whose lives are dependent on you. Robin is a highly principled person with great integrity. He has already been a fine member of his family because he has accomplished much and he's done it all himself.

The Russells have played an important role in society going back many generations. The family origins can be traced back to Stephen Russell, who represented Weymouth in Parliament in 1394. He was the great-great-grandfather of John Russell, who became the first Earl of Bedford and established the family fortune. His rise to fame and power was impressively fast. After serving in the army of Henry VIII in France, he was knighted for valour in 1522. He became one of the six gentlemen of the Privy Chamber, two of whom slept each night in the king's bedroom, and was entrusted with many diplomatic missions. He was made Lord High Admiral and his banner, which was to become the family's permanent coat of arms, was exhibited for the first time. The family motto '*Che Sera Sera*', 'Whatever Will Be Will Be', dates from the second earl.

He found equal favour with the new king, Edward VI, who gave him Woburn Abbey in 1547. Henry VIII had ordered his commissioners to seize the abbey nine years previously at the general dissolution of the monasteries.

The abbey, which had been built in 1145, was for the first 400 years of its life occupied by monks. For the next 400 it was to be occupied in various degrees of comfort by the Russell family.

Sir John's fortune did not stop at Woburn. Three years later he was created the first Earl of Bedford and given more land in Devon and Cornwall. A few years after that he was given the Covent Garden site and seven acres in Long Acre in London which were sold by the eleventh duke just before the First World War.

Woburn was not lived in by the second or third earls. Francis, the fourth earl, however, decided to make it into a home. He arranged for most of the old abbey to be rebuilt, with advice from Inigo Jones. The fourth earl was also responsible for the Piazza on the Covent Garden Estate and made a major contribution to English agriculture by draining the Fens.

The fifth earl provided the family with its dukedom. His son William, Lord Russell was ordered to be executed for treason by Charles II. As a form of compensation for the loss of his son, the fifth earl was created Duke of Bedford and Marquess of Tavistock by William and Mary, who also reversed his son's condemnation and ordered that the matter be obliterated from all official records.

Before William, Lord Russell died he none the less managed to make a substantial contribution to the family by marrying the daughter of the Earl of Southampton who as part of her dowry brought Bloomsbury to the Russell family.

The second duke added a title to the family name by marrying, at fourteen, thirteen-year-old Elizabeth Howland. She came from a family of rich merchants and in order to preserve the name, the barony of Howland was created for the Russell family. Andrew, as the first son of the Marquess of Tavistock, is known as Lord Howland. Robbie and Jamie are respectively Lord Robin Russell and Lord James Russell. The third duke, unlike his father, did not increase the family fortune as he was a compulsive gambler.

Other Russells have contributed to both the family and society. The first duke became involved in building first the dry and then the wet dock at Rotherhithe. John, the fourth duke, held many high offices including First Lord of the Admiralty and was regarded as a naval hero. He later became Principal Secretary of State and ambassador to France. He negotiated the Treaty of Paris in 1763. He refurbished Woburn Abbey with the help of the architect Henry Flitcroft and bought much of the china and furniture still there today.

Francis, the fifth duke, was a man who lived in great style, although he never married. He called in the famous architect Henry Holland and modified many of the rooms at Woburn. He also transformed the Woburn farmlands into one of the most productive and well-managed estates in England and founded the family's racing interests.

John, the sixth duke, redressed the balance by marrying twice and producing nine sons and three daughters. His third son, Lord John Russell, won a national reputation for his championing of the Parliamentary Reform Bill. He served as Prime Minister in 1846-52 and 1865-6 and continued to promote liberal reform in the Whig Party, as well as religious freedom, democratisation of town governments and state support of public education. The philosopher Bertrand Russell was the grandson of the sixth duke's third son. Hastings, the ninth duke, was an ardent agriculturalist and astute businessman. Herbrand, the eleventh duke, and Robin's great-grandfather, was a forbidding man who had a highly developed sense of public duty. He lived a cold, aloof existence isolated from the outside world by a mass of servants. His only concern was the administration of the estates.

Despite his wife having a personal income of £30,000 a year, and four maids, she was not a spender. When Ian Bedford wrote to her in desperation asking for £3 to buy three shirts, she refused, castigating him for his extravagance.

The eleventh duke helped run the household, which included drawing up the lunch and dinner menus. He was however a man of few words. He had wanted a large family but after the traumatic birth of their first child, later to be the twelfth duke, his wife never had another.

She and the duke were walking by themselves on a deserted moor four days before Christmas 1888 when she suddenly realised her baby was about to be born. There was no doctor or midwife around, but they found a shepherd's derelict cottage. There, the young duchess, used to raising a finger for a footman to fetch a chair, lay down on some heather and gave birth.

During her marriage she was left entirely to her own devices and developed her own interests. She was a member of the Skating Club in Knightsbridge and when she heard that the owner was going to sell the rink, persuaded her husband to buy up the lease of the club so that she might continue to skate.

She also founded a hospital at Battlesden, near the village of Woburn. The patients were poor and the duchess liked to attend and help at every operation no matter what time of the day or night, a practice she maintained even after the hospital was taken over by the army at the outbreak of the First World War. She often worked as many as sixteen hours a day. She also drew up plans for another small hospital called Maryland in the village of Woburn, which still exists today.

She became a first-class shot and once shot 272 pheasants in four and a half hours. She refused to be driven by a chauffeur and carried out her own car repairs, including changing tyres at the side of the road.

Perhaps most remarkable of all, she took up flying at the age of sixty-two and took part in a number of record-breaking flights to India and South Africa. This remarkable woman became known as the 'Flying Duchess'. In 1937, when she was seventy-one, she took

Henrietta's father, merchant banker Henry Tiarks, with her mother the actress Joan Barry in 1938, the year they married.

Robin in 1940 aged six months, with his mother Clare and his father Lord Howland, who subsequently became the 13th Duke of Bedford.

Henrietta aged fifteen months with her mother, 1941.

Below left   Robin aged four with his mother outside their home in Wilton Street, London SW1, in 1944, approximately two years before she died.

Below right   Henrietta aged five with her mother outside their home, 69, Avenue Road, London NW8, 1945.

Henrietta aged seven with her grandfather merchant banker Frank
Tiarks in the garden of her home, 1947.

Henrietta and Robin aged six, 1946.

Robin aged ten in South Africa where his father bought a 200-acre apricot farm near Cape Town, 1950.

Henrietta aged eleven with her mother the day Margaret Sweeney married the Duke of Argyll, 1951. *Copyright Portman Press Bureau*

Robin aged fifteen at Le Rosey school in Switzerland in 1955 where he met his life-long friend Chuck Downer. He had already talked to Henrietta about getting married.

This photograph of Henrietta aged sixteen in 1956 by Anthony
Armstrong Jones (later Lord Snowdon), started the competition
'Is This the Most Beautiful Girl in Britain?' *Copyright Snowdon*

Henrietta and Robin's wedding day, 21 June 1961. Top left the groom's brother Lord Rudolph Russell, his father the Duke of Bedford, the bride's friend, Countess Bunny Esterhazy, Robin, Henrietta, the best man Viscount Chelsea, second from the right the bride's father Henry Tiarks. Sitting right, the bride's mother, sitting left the Duke's third wife Nicole. The photograph was taken at Claridge's. *Copyright Tom Hustler*

The bride and groom leaving the reception. *Copyright Tom Hustler*

Above left Henrietta and Robin with their first child Andrew, aged four months, when they were re-united with him on their return to England from their year in Boston, USA, 1962. *Copyright Keystone Press Agency Limited*

Above right Robin and Henrietta at Woburn, Christmas Eve, 1962.

Andrew, three, Robbie eighteen months, on holiday at Henrietta's parents' home in Montego Bay, Jamaica, 1965.

off to complete 200 hours of solo flying. She was about an hour short. A snowstorm blew up and she was never seen again. Her plane was washed up on the shore at Yarmouth. There is a room dedicated to her at Woburn and in her memory a 'Fly-In' is held at Woburn every year when Tiger Moths from all over the world fly into Woburn for a rally.

The twelfth duke had a lonely and unhappy childhood. There were no other children at Woburn and he had only the deer for company. He did not get on with his father, grew up to be a self-centred and cold man and broke off relations with his father just before the First World War. They had no contact for over twenty years. He was a pacifist who loved birds and animals and became very unpopular during the Second World War when he made pacifist speeches in the House of Lords. His marriage to Louisa Whitwell was not a happy one and he paid little attention to his wife and three children, Ian, his heir, Hugh and Daphne. Robin's father had almost no family life. He knew nothing of his background. He had no idea that the Duke of Bedford was the head of his family until a parlourmaid told him when he was sixteen, which was also the age he first saw Woburn.

When Ian was a teenager, the eleventh duke altered the way Woburn and the estate had been administered. In future there was to be no automatic inheritance. Instead a group of trustees would have total power to choose who inherited from among the 300 descendants of the sixth duke.

Ian's father was very mean, their house in Havant was kept bitterly cold except for the aviaries which were full of valuable birds. Ian would creep in there to warm up on particularly cold days. Although his father received an allowance of £13,500 a year, he gave Ian's mother only £1,500 a year to clothe herself and their three children, pay the wages of eight servants and settle all the household bills. Ian used to be dressed in clothes that were too big or too small.

In 1935 his parents went through a public legal separation. His mother sued his father for restitution of conjugal rights, saying that he had deserted her. His father pleaded that he was justified in refusing to cohabit with his wife. The case was the talk of London at the time. The end of the marriage also marked the end of Ian's relationship with his mother.

*　　*　　*

Meanwhile eighteen-year-old Robin, who wanted to be a good duke, had decided it would be a good idea for him and Henrietta to marry.

'We knew each other incredibly well,' he explained, 'and I thought I loved her. But I only thought it. I didn't know it because I didn't know what love was all about. Henrietta did. She'd been very loved at home and was more mature than I was. I thought we should try getting married and if it didn't work, we could split up. I didn't think I would ever be very happy. I didn't think I deserved to be happy.'

Parental objection intervened, however, and the two parted. 'At first I missed her a lot, but then I decided to get on with my life and between eighteen and twenty we both had other friends.'

Robin decided he wanted to go to Harvard mainly because Chuck Downer was going there. He didn't tell his father but went over to the United States, slept on the floor of a friend's room at Harvard, went to a crammer and took the Scholastic Aptitude Test which was an entry requirement. He was thrilled when he heard he had passed and rang his father to tell him the good news.

His father responded by saying that with his family background and connections, he was bound to have got in.

At Harvard he met up again with Chuck and they shared a room together. 'Robin used to get up much earlier than I did,' Chuck remembers, 'and every morning would go out and bring me back coffee and doughnuts. Karim and Amyn Aga Khan, Robin's cousins by marriage, were there too and we had great fun together. Henrietta was often in Robin's thoughts. I used to be against her. I thought she was too pushy, too concerned with social things, especially during all that coming-out period.'

Robin remembers clearly the day Henrietta knocked on his door and asked for their relationship to be given another chance. 'I told her that if we tried again, she would have to be worthy of me and that to be a good wife she had to be faithful and loyal. I told her she had to prove she was worth returning to. But the confidence I showed on the outside wasn't what I felt inside. I have always had a complex about myself, a total lack of confidence, and I wanted her approval of my life. I wanted her to keep telling me I was doing very well. I think it stems from my father who was always telling me I wasn't doing well. My ego was terrible. I needed her to boost it all the time. But of course I didn't tell her that.'

Chuck thinks that Henrietta has always had a tremendous influence in Robin's life. 'I think he may have seen a certain maternal streak in her. He always dominated their relationship outwardly, but beneath the surface she was the one who guided things. I think most women do. When Robin was twenty-one his godfather, Lord Beaverbrook, gave him $5,000 as a birthday present. I wanted to go off with him on holiday but he used the money to go and see Henrietta. However, when they finally did get married I was converted pretty quickly to believing she was a super woman and have been a devotee ever since.

'I think Robin finds it very hard to give love and loved her as much as he was capable. Robin has a cold exterior that he finds extremely difficult to break through. But that coldness is a protective shell against any more hurt. He suffered so much at a crucial age. Inside that shell is the nicest, sweetest man that ever lived. He has a heart of gold, he's considerate, kind and everything you would want in a person.

'I think he was also attracted to Henrietta's strength which subconsciously he recognised he needed. He is, in some ways, extremely strong and has a discipline I have rarely seen in anyone. But he is basically an insecure person, whereas Henrietta is not and I think Robin fed on that strength. The root of Robin's problems probably goes back several generations. Ian Bedford suffered enormously at the hands of his parents and grandparents. Robin didn't have a warm family life with his parents either. These are the things you pass on to your children without meaning to.'

After Robin and Henrietta were married Robin hid his lack of confidence by deliberately being a forceful husband. 'I made Henrietta recook meals and change her clothes if I didn't like what she was wearing, because I thought my standards had to be high to impress her,' he said. 'I wasn't prepared to accept anything less because she had a spoilt upbringing and I felt I had to bring her into line a bit. However, in those days you couldn't be too strong with Henrietta. She had a wonderful disposition. If I said "No" to something, she would come back two days later and try again. Sometimes I would change my mind. I was also strict when we first got married because I wanted to become first in her life. Her parents were first initially. I often threatened to leave her, although of course I never would. I know I worked too hard. I had to prove myself to the trustees and my father. The trustees could have left Woburn to any of about three hundred descendants of the sixth duke and I wanted to make sure it was left to me. I persuaded them to alter the documents in the sixties so that I and then my children would inherit the estate.

'I love Woburn and have never wanted the estate to be sold. It meant I worked as hard as I could, as well as I could, as fast as I could, to impress them. I know I was very difficult and I hope the last two years since my stroke have made Henrietta realise that I'm now dramatically better. In those days I used to be too disciplined and I hope that now life is a little easier for her. She's a wonderful lady to be married to, but you have to be on your toes all the time. You can never get away with anything and never take her for granted.'

Chapter 5

Marriage and Motherhood

In marriage as in literature, the whole art consists in the grace of transitions.   Honoré de Balzac

Henrietta

Once I became a mother I stopped throwing childish tantrums, but although we were now a family, my parents were still able to manipulate me. Soon after we had had Andrew my mother said that it would be better for the baby to be in London rather than in our small flat in Boston. I don't know why Robin and I agreed to it. I suppose we listened because we were so young. Now I see how totally unnecessary it was.

When Andrew was eight weeks old, the maternity nurse took him back to England to live with my parents. I stayed with Robin while he took his final exams. I'll never forget how awful it was to see my baby being taken away. I was absolutely terrified that the plane would crash. Andrew and I were apart for about eight weeks. I missed him terribly.

My mother persuaded the Bedford trustees that the best place for Robin and me to live after we came back from America was in Clarendon Place, a terrace of houses just being built round the corner from where she and Daddy lived. The trustees agreed and we just fell in with the plans. From that June until the following March while the five-bedroomed house was being built we lived with my parents. I thought Mummy was amazing because she said we were to do just what we wanted. I wasn't sensitive enough to realise that it was a

59

very difficult time for Robin because in my home my parents still felt they had control of me.

We didn't see much of my in-laws and when we did I didn't get on very well with them. Robin and I were both worried that as Robin was Ian's heir, if we were ever killed Ian would insist on bringing Andrew up. So to prevent this happening, we named our friends Marybelle and Jamie Drummond his guardians.

Of course Mummy helped me choose the décor of our new house and we had an internal line installed between our house and hers. At the time I didn't mind at all. Family tensions increased, however, soon after we moved in. Mummy liked to pop in a lot and when Robin came back from the office, Mummy would often be there. He became very sullen and one day when she'd left he said, 'I never want your mother around when I come back from the office again.' I had to tell her that. It was terribly hard for her because she really wanted Robin to love her but looking at it now, they were both trying to assert their control over me at the same time.

Robin used to complain about my parents a lot and say, 'You've either got to be their daughter or my wife. You can't be both.' And my mother would complain about Robin. She had always liked him, but was worried that he was obviously so insecure. It was very difficult for a long time. Eventually I got to the point where I plucked up my courage and said to both of them, 'Tell each other your complaints, don't tell me. I don't care what you think about each other. I love you all and this is untenable.' But I had been married for at least twelve years before I dared to do it.

Andrew was one when we moved into Clarendon Place. By then I'd also had a miscarriage and was pregnant again with Robbie, who was born on 12 August 1963.

I think the first few years of any marriage are the most difficult. There's such a lot of adjustment and Robin and I had some tough times. He was often difficult to communicate with. One of the problems was that he always used to drive himself too hard. He was determined to succeed. He had to prove to his father that he could get to the top. He longed for his father to say, 'I admire you. Well done.' He started training as a chartered accountant, but didn't enjoy it so he went and worked for a stockbroker. He picked a company that he knew did no business with Schroder's, the merchant bank my father was a director of, because he didn't want Ian Bedford to say my father had got him the job. Then he went to work for the very good firm of stockbrokers De Zoete & Bevan, and also became a director of a number of companies.

I spent a lot of time thinking about marriage. I realised that when a couple get to an impasse in an argument, one person has got to give in and that there are many people who are incapable of saying sorry. Robin is very stubborn and I discovered quite early on that the easiest thing to do, even if I was absolutely convinced that something was his fault, was for me to apologise. When I did, that was the end of it. He'd say, 'That's perfectly all right, darling,' and on we went again. If I didn't apologise, we could be at loggerheads for days.

I don't believe in men equally sharing the domestic load. It's very nice if a man is helpful in the house, but I think it's awful for a man to do the washing-up. That is not what men are for and I think it alters the balance of the relationship.

I think men are basically the providers and when they are at home, they should be looked after. I think a man should be looked up to and, even if his wife has a lot of influence, his decision should be final, particularly in front of the children. I also decided that one of the reasons why marriages went wrong was that most men got up very early and worked all day, whereas their wives often had the opportunity of staying in bed quite late or having a rest in the afternoon. When their husbands came home from work, they would be tired but the wives would want to go out to dinner and on to a night-club. I felt it was important to lead a life parallel to one's husband. That way if he was tired, you'd be tired. So I used to get up very early with Robin and drive him to the office just after 7.00 a.m. We didn't have a chauffeur until after Jamie was born. We left that early because Robin liked to get to the office before 8.00 a.m. to work peacefully before anyone else arrived. And at the end of his day the children and I often went to fetch him.

I drove him for at least five years. Robin was always grumpy in the mornings and never appreciated what I was doing. One morning we pulled up alongside a chauffeur-driven Rolls. We both looked at the man reading *The Times* in the back seat and Robin said, 'Wouldn't it be wonderful to go to the office like that?' I was angry and hurt and I said, 'I bet he'd envy you if you told him that your wife drove you to work every morning.'

On another occasion we were driving down the Embankment and Robin turned to me and said, 'Tell me exactly what you think you contribute to our marriage.' I pulled in to the side of the road and said, 'Maybe between now and when you get to the office you'll work it out.' I dropped him off and never drove him to the office again.

David Wolfson who lived two doors away said that morning after morning he would see me drive into the garage after I had dropped Robin off, with tears streaming down my face. When I get angry, it's all very open, as it is when I'm sad or happy. Robin keeps things inside him.

I used to behave quite differently when Robin was around. I became tense and looked around frantically in case there was something he might not like. I have always hated incurring his displeasure.

Sometimes in those early days our relationship got so bad I'd think: I can't cope any longer. What made me love him and always stay, even though there were times when the whole thing could have ended, was that I knew that how he appeared from the outside was not how he really was on the inside. In fact it is only now after his stroke that I feel I'm married to the person that I knew was inside him all the time. It's as if the real Robin was camouflaged for all those years.

I never liked living in London and in a way I feel my married life really began when we bought our country home at Chevington near Newmarket in 1968.

We had been talking about having a house in the country and I used to buy *Country Life* and look at all the houses. In fact it is still something I love to do. One day Robin arranged to have the magazine delivered to the house and in that first issue, I saw a picture of a really pretty white Georgian house with a pond and a cedar tree. It looked so magical that I rushed downstairs to Robin who was having breakfast and showed it to him. He looked at it and said, 'I'm not surprised you think it's lovely, it's only ten miles from Newmarket.' We already had horses in training there.

Curiously I hadn't actually noticed where it was. He told me to take my mother with me if I was going to look at it because he knew she had very good taste and wouldn't be seduced by the fact that it was near Newmarket.

Mummy and I drove down to see it. As we drove up the drive she said, 'Stop. There's no point in going in. In my experience houses as pretty as that on the outside are dreadful inside.' I took no notice and we went in. We'd only seen three rooms when Mummy whispered, 'You've got to have it. It's wonderful.' I didn't know the procedure of buying a house. I rang the agent straightaway and said, 'I think we'd like to have it.' The agent said, 'Do you mean you'll accept the asking price?' I didn't even know what it was. He told me it was £35,000. I said, 'Yes.'

Driving back to London I realised that I'd said we'd buy it and Robin hadn't even seen it. When I got home I told him how wonderful it was and we arranged to go and see it that coming Saturday. We drove down and as Robin's sense of direction isn't wonderful, we got a little bit lost. The light started flashing on our car, indicating that we were low on petrol. Robin said he wouldn't fill up until after we'd seen the house and that if we ran out of petrol before we arrived, it meant we wouldn't buy it. Luckily we didn't run out. I was incredibly nervous and hoped he would like it. He walked round with absolutely no expression on his face at all. He didn't say one word until we had nearly returned to London. I forced myself to keep quiet. I knew it would be wrong to push him. Finally he said he thought it was a very nice house and to my delight the trustees bought it for us.

They also suggested that as Robin had become involved in running 10,000 acres of the estates at Woburn, we ought to have a base in the village and we lived in a house in Marquis Court from 1970. Ian had Woburn Abbey and forty acres, but had nothing to do with the rest of the estate.

Our new house in Chevington, which we called Chevington Russell, had ten bedrooms, some stables, three small thatched cottages in the grounds and a duckpond. The garden was very pretty but rather overgrown. We got possession of it in April 1968 and spent a marvellous first weekend there with the friends we had chosen to be our children's guardians, Marybelle and Jamie Drummond.

From the moment we had the house it felt like home. I don't think we could have made Woburn Abbey into the home it has become if we had not first made our base at Chevington. There was an Aga in the kitchen which at first I wanted to get rid of but Marybelle said, 'Just cook on it for one weekend first.' And of course she was right. It was fantastic. I'd love to have one at Woburn, but sadly we can't because the kitchen chimney is too tall to draw properly.

We looked forward to furnishing the house. There were lots of outlying buildings full of furniture at Woburn, including many items that came from the wing that was knocked down by the fifth duke because it was full of dry rot. As none of the furniture was in the abbey itself, we thought it would be wonderful to use some of it. Robin's father was away so Robin talked to the trustees who agreed we could take it from Woburn.

We filled a furniture van with things we liked and took it down to the house. But it wasn't there long. When my father-in-law returned from his trip, he took every bit back. He said he needed it all.

At the time I was really angry and thought he was being unreasonable. Thinking about it now, I would be just as angry as my father-in-law was if any of my children did the same. I'm actually now quite grateful to him because slowly, over the years we lived at Chevington, we accumulated some lovely things. The sixties was a very good time for buying antique furniture.

We later bought fifty-six acres of land around the house and fenced it for a stud farm and built six cottages for the stud hands.

We had friends down at weekends. One year David and Jeni Sieff spent thirty weekends with us and lots of other friends came for the races and sales at Newmarket. It is particularly nice to have a house where people come for a specific reason like the races or sales, because you know they really want to be there.

Paul Ford, who used to be a freelance chauffeur in London, and whom we knew well, came and lived in one of the cottages and helped us run the house. He also drove the tractor and mowed the paddocks.

We had a gardener, whose wife was our daily, and a cook who used to come in at weekends. I also did a lot of cooking myself.

We reared a pet lamb for the children in memory of the lamb my grandfather let me look after when I was six or seven. We called her Emma. We all had jerseys knitted from her wool and she lived until she was thirteen.

Robin and I loved the house and so did our children and friends. It was bliss, a dream world that was abruptly shattered one Friday night in January 1973. Robin drove down from his work in London on Friday evenings for the weekend. This particular Friday he came straight into the drawing-room and asked the children to leave the room so he could speak to me. I wondered what on earth I had done wrong.

He asked me if I'd like a drink, which I refused, so he said, 'I think you're going to need one.' I asked for a whisky. He came back with whisky that was tea-coloured. As he handed it to me I was thinking: He wouldn't have offered me a drink if he was angry with me. Then he began. 'What I'm going to tell you is going to upset you a lot. My father is emigrating and I'm going to have to go and live at Woburn because I've got to run it. But I remember my promise to you when we got married that you'd never have to live there, so I'll come back and see you as often as I can.'

I burst into tears. I felt our life was being torn apart. I didn't want to go to Woburn. I also felt that if Robin went to Woburn without me, it meant he didn't need me. I wrote Ian a terrible letter saying he was ruining our lives. He in turn wrote me an awful letter back. Ian said that by leaving Woburn he was making a huge sacrifice for Robin because unless you moved into Woburn when you were young, you wouldn't have the energy or the will to cope with it. I've discovered that he was right, but I don't believe that was his reason. I think he left because he didn't get on with the trustees and disliked having to work with them. He particularly disliked the fact that Robin, who was running the main part of the estate, got on with them very well.

I can't say I hate Ian. In a funny sort of way we admire a lot about each other. Since Robin's stroke we probably get on better than we ever have. I think we've both mellowed and respect each other now. I also know he can't hurt Robin any more. He's never been able to hurt me even when he mentioned the possibility of my having a Down's Syndrome child, although he has made me extremely angry. But I have always hated him hurting the people I love – Robin and my parents.

There was a year between our knowing we were going to Woburn and actually moving in. It was a very negative year. There was no point in continuing with our life at Chevington Russell as it was, because that was coming to an end. And we weren't at Woburn so couldn't plan anything there either.

We were invited to join Ian and Nicole for their last Christmas at Woburn. We didn't usually spend Christmas with them and agreed rather reluctantly. When we drove up to the house on Christmas Day; I thought it odd that there were two television generator trucks outside. I assumed that as Nicole was so organised she'd probably got some elaborate entertainment arranged that needed back-up power. Finlay, Ian's butler, opened the door and took us up to the drawing-room and said, as we walked through the ante-library, 'Remember that once you walk in that room you're on camera.' I didn't really grasp what he'd said until he opened the door and I saw the hot TV lights and cameras. The whole thing was being filmed for a television special called *A Farewell to Woburn*.

I was furious because we hadn't been told in advance. The children were filmed opening their presents and we were all filmed eating Christmas dinner in the Canaletto room. I had come for a family Christmas and found the whole thing so intrusive that I didn't behave too well. Robin, however, behaved beautifully, although underneath he too was furious.

66

Ian and Nicole finally left Woburn on 3 April 1974. Nicole was as miserable about leaving as I was about going there. Because it was so hard for them to go, I think they pretended that they were just going on a trip as nothing at all had been packed. All their clothes were left in the cupboards.

I arrived the next day from Chevington with a trailer with the children, my favourite possessions, plus the ducks and sheep. Goodness knows what they all thought of us at the abbey as we arrived. We must have looked like the Beverly Hillbillies in comparison.

Robin's car broke down twice coming from London to Woburn and he didn't arrive until very late. I was sure it was an omen. I had asked Robin if we could sleep in his old room, the one we always used when we visited the house but he said, 'No, we're going to sleep in my father's room.' I didn't want to and argued with him, until he said finally, 'Well, you can sleep in our old room, but I'm sleeping in Dad's room. If you live in the house that's the room you sleep in.' I did as I was told, but for at least a year I felt I was trespassing and that Nicole was going to walk in at any second and ask me what I was doing in her bed.

It took a year for Finlay to pack. He started in the dressing-room with Ian's clothes, then packed the linen. We had to buy everything new. Then the lamps went. And so on. Meanwhile everything happened as though they were still there. Nobody asked us what we wanted, meals just appeared. My bath was run every day at the time Nicole liked to have her bath run, regardless of what time I wanted it. I longed to put up a sign that said, 'Under new management'.

There were nine or ten personal staff, but two hundred altogether involved in the running of Woburn. I saw dozens of people every day and at first I didn't know any of their names or what they were doing. I think it was as difficult for them as for us.

After a month I got quite brave and I moved something. The next day it was back in the same place. That went on for two or three days until I was told by Finlay that Her Grace had put the object where it was because that's where it should be.

Woburn was a thriving business that ran on its own momentum. All the people running it kept on doing the things they'd always done. Neither Robin nor I had had any experience that could have equipped us for the job ahead.

Ian used to sell in the shop every weekend and we started doing that. I found it embarrassing because I could be standing behind a counter and people would come up, look at me and say, 'Ooh, she's not as tall as I thought she was, is she, Mabel?' It was as though I was a Madame Tussaud's waxwork. I hated it and I don't do it any more.

My father-in-law was a wonderful showman and as he walked around the house he used to chat to everybody, and autograph postcards and guidebooks. I find that sort of thing embarrassing too. Of course if I'm going through the house to do something and I meet visitors on the way, I say, 'Good morning' or 'I hope you're having a nice time' but I can't just walk around to be seen. The one thing I happily did that Ian used to do was spend a lot of time picking up litter. That made more sense because I felt at least I was doing something useful.

The duke had in fact made a tremendous success of running Woburn as a stately home. Because nearly £7 million death duties were owed on the death of his father, the trustees had wanted the National Trust to take over the property leaving the duke as tenant. He'd fought against this as he was determined to keep Woburn in the family's hands. 'I felt that if Woburn was sold or otherwise disposed of to the National Trust or some institution, something would have gone out of the family and indeed the history of England, which could possibly never be replaced,' he said in his autobiography *A Silver-Plated Spoon*.

When he took over, the abbey had not been lived in since the eleventh duke died, thirteen years previously. It was filthy and in a shocking state of disrepair.

'I soon realised,' he said, 'that the only way of financing the reopening of the house would be to follow the example of other families in our position and allow the public to see it in return for an entrance fee. The trustees had distinct reservations about the whole idea, but to me the whole future of the family and indeed its right to exist in the second half of the twentieth century was bound up with the reopening of Woburn. I wanted people to enjoy themselves, give them service and value for money and make sure they would come back again. If this enabled me to live in my ancestral home, then everyone would be satisfied.' He and his second wife Lydia cleaned and restored much of the property themselves.

'One advantage was that we were starting from scratch,' he said. 'We worked like dogs. Every room was filthy. We used to work all day, camping out in the vast house, boiling up water for morning coffee in an electric kettle and then going out to the Bedford Arms in the village for a warm meal in the evening. My father had removed the whole kitchen block and there was nowhere to cook.'

They made the remarkable find of a priceless set of Sèvres porcelain, which had been given to the wife of the fourth duke by Louis XV, lying all over the floor in loose boxes in one of the stable blocks. Because of its value he and Lydia carefully washed it themselves, all 800-odd pieces of it. The paintings, too, were kept rather oddly. Every picture the family possessed was stacked on the floor in rows about twelve feet deep along the wall in the Long Gallery. The shifting and processing were spread over months.

Untold hours were spent in the Grotto on the ground floor of the Inigo Jones wing, scrubbing the ormer shells and stone stalagmites with nail-brushes and Lux. 'I think we used fifty packets,' he said. The duke had made up his mind to open the abbey to the public in April 1955, which gave him just six months to get everything sorted out. There was a desperate last-minute rush to tar access roads and mark out car park sites.

It was a success right from the start with 181,000 visitors during that first year. The house has one of the most important private art collections in the world and Ian set up a children's zoo, playground and boating lake.

The duke developed a keen eye for publicity and Woburn was once home to a nudist convention. Running Woburn occupied his time and energy. When he married Nicole in 1960, he told her that Woburn Abbey came first.

Over the years various attractions were added, including a wildlife park which was opened in May 1970. Nicole had the stables converted to look like streets which were then lined with antique shops and have become a very successful antiques centre. They opened two restaurants, a buffet and a banqueting department. Henrietta and Robin were left a massive enterprise to run.

Henrietta
Robin and I soon realised how grateful we were to Ian for being such a showman and putting Woburn on the map. It meant Robin and I could afford the luxury of being more private people. I was, however, very unhappy during the first few months at Woburn. I spent one whole night writing down all the reasons why it was pointless, hopeless and horrible living in a house like Woburn. I gave it to Robin to read, but I don't think he ever did, so I put it away and haven't looked at it since. I was rebellious and really miserable – a nightmare. I'm like that with things I can't cope with.

But after a year Finlay finished packing and went to join the duke, and things started to improve. Most of the domestic staff left too because we weren't living the way they'd been used to. It meant we could employ new people and run the house our way.

A wonderful cook called Mrs Cook who had been at Woburn when Robin was a child and Lydia the duchess, came back. So did Ernest, who'd been the butler when Lydia was there and had been with the Queen Mother in the interim. So in a way Woburn became like we'd known it when we were children.

The first really good thing to happen after moving to Woburn, was Jamie. Robin had always told me that two children were enough and that I could not have any more unless I was of breeding age and we lived at Woburn, which he was sure was not going to happen.

I actually think that if I had had two girls he wouldn't have thought it was enough. I reminded him of his promise. We moved into Woburn on 4 April 1974 and Jamie was born on 11 February 1975.

I always wanted a girl and always had the names ready. Andrew would have been Elizabeth, Robbie would have been Charlotte, and Jamie, Victoria. Now, however, I'm delighted I have three boys.

Chapter 6

Life with the Horses

Happiness is a knack like whistling through your fingers.

Mark Twain

Henrietta

Apart from my family, horses have been the things I have loved most all my life. I read horse books endlessly when I was a child and first rode when I was about three. Daddy bought me my first horse when I was thirteen. I called her Foxtrot, after a horse in one of the many horse books I read.

Although I adored having a horse, I was never a very brave rider. I think my father was sad about that and even my mother was disappointed at my lack of competitiveness. I remember once taking part in a gymkhana and Mummy calling out to me, 'Go on! Go faster!' My answer was 'My pony doesn't want to go any faster.' I loved watching other people ride, however, and it was always a treat when I stayed with my grandfather and he took me to the Bath and West Show.

I think the first seeds of my interest in racehorses were sown when I was about eight or nine. I was travelling to New York on the *Queen Mary* and watched a film about a racehorse called Sea Biscuit. It made me think about how much I would like to breed a racehorse of my own, perhaps even a champion.

Some years later I read a book and realised that all thoroughbreds were descended from three stallions and about twenty mares. It was fascinating because it meant that all

71

pedigrees were traceable and that to breed a thoroughbred one could study the generations of both the sire and the dam and design one's own pattern to hopefully breed a champion horse. It made me want to breed racehorses even more. I liked the idea that if I bred a champion, he would not have existed but for me.

After Robin and I were married, I felt that I would like to contribute something of my own to the Russell family. It didn't take me long to work out the most suitable area. I discovered that the fifth duke founded the Bedford racing interests. He bred three Derby winners in the late eighteenth century. The involvement was sustained by the seventh duke, but after that there had not been much family interest in either breeding or racing. I felt I wanted to make their renowned colours famous again. When we reregistered them they had not been seen on the racecourse for over one hundred years. I felt it would be wonderful to see the purple and white stripes and black velvet cap with gold tassel on a winner – maybe one day even on another Derby winner.

I bought my first filly foal in 1965. She cost 700 guineas and I called her Irania. Robin was against my buying her, but didn't actually say that I couldn't. I hoped she would become our first racehorse, but she didn't. I didn't realise when I bought her that her front legs were not those of an athlete at all.

The following year I bought a yearling and although Robin was no longer quite so disapproving, he remained uninterested. I, meanwhile, had become intrigued about pedigrees and bloodlines. Because Karim Aga Khan and Robin had been brought up as cousins, I had already absorbed a lot about the Aga Khan's horses which have some of the most interesting bloodlines in the world. I studied and learned as much as I could.

The following year I went up to Newmarket for the yearling sales. I had wanted to stay all week, but I had to come back on Thursday as it was Nanny's day off. When I got back to London, Robin said to me, 'By the way, I'm getting up very early tomorrow morning because I'm going to the sales.' I couldn't believe it and was very irritated. Thursday and Friday were the days when the best horses were sold. I asked him to look at a filly for me and gave him the lot number. When he came home he was very excited because not only had he bought the filly, but he had been persuaded to join a syndicate of ten and had bought a yearling. The yearling was called Rodrigo, was by Charlottesville and had been sold for the then record price of 31,000 guineas. The amount amazed me, as I had seen him earlier in the week and hadn't been impressed. Robin was particularly pleased that Rodrigo would be trained by Vincent O'Brien. The horse, however, never set foot on a racecourse. Robin had wasted his money and it really put him off, particularly as the three horses we had bought were no good either.

I, on the other hand, was by then completely hooked. Robin gave me my first horse-box and when I drove it, it felt just as good, if not better, than I had imagined it would feel as a child. However, after I had the children, I totally lost my nerve to ride. I have always been aware that a horse is much more in control of me than I am of it.

Although the three horses we had bought were not going to run, we could, at least, still breed from them. We sold their progeny at the Newmarket sales, but they realised very little. The only good investment we made in the early days was to buy a share in a racehorse called Reform.

This meant we could send a mare to be covered by him every year, or we could sell the right to someone else. Fortunately Reform was a very good horse and the nominations to him sold well. I sold our nomination every year and Robin only allowed me to use the amount we got to cover all the mares we had. He refused to allow me to spend any more. I am so glad he did this because it forced me to learn about value. I discovered that buying the most expensive horses does not necessarily mean buying the best. You can find good horses quite cheaply, but it requires effort, knowledge, learning and above all luck.

During the next fourteen years, we only had one winner and that was of a minor race at Windsor. Those years weren't easy, but in retrospect I'm very pleased they weren't, because when something good happens now, I realise just how precious and difficult it is to achieve.

I began to go to Tattersalls' sales at Newmarket which is

probably one of the best places in the world to buy horses. And I have been every year without fail since 1966.

Before I set off, Robin always used to say to me, 'Don't you dare buy anything.' That was very good for me too because I spent a long time looking at the horses and learning what to look for. I took it very seriously and always marked up all my catalogues as if I was buying. There also wasn't a stallion standing in England or a public stud that I didn't visit. I can fill in a five-generation pedigree form like other people do a crossword puzzle.

The next development came a few years after we bought Chevington, our country home. Robin bought fifty acres around the house to turn into a stud farm. Unfortunately Ian Bedford left Woburn and we had to abandon our plans. I was very unhappy at the time, but little did I know how my whole life would change a year after we moved into Woburn. That year, 1975, was a particularly special one because Jamie was born in February and Mrs Moss came into my life in December.

The autumn before I bought Mrs Moss was a lucky one. We had drawn a nomination in the National Stud ballot to send a mare to Grundy, the winner of the 1975 Derby. There had been so many people wanting a nomination that the only way was to ballot, and we were one of the lucky ones. Robin felt that the mares we already had were not good enough to send and suggested I bought one specially. I didn't need telling twice and went to the December sales.

I arrived early in the morning. I sat in the ring talking to Grundy's co-breeder. I was asking him what he thought I should look for that would suit Grundy when Mrs Moss walked into the ring. She was by Reform and I instantly loved her. I looked at the catalogue to confirm that she had an acceptable pedigree. She had. The bidding was sticking at £1,900 and it was obvious she hadn't reached the reserve. I have absolutely no recollection of thinking: I will bid, but my hand must have gone up because the hammer dropped and they said my name. She had cost 2,100 guineas. I panicked. Robin had told me I could buy only one mare and it was to be a good one. I had been allowed to spend 12,000 guineas, but I had bought one for far less, that would never be accepted by the National Stud for Grundy.

I ran out of the ring to look at her. She had a club-foot. I thought: This is a disaster. What am I going to do? I rushed round to my friend Keith Freeman, one of the leading bloodstock agents, and asked him if he could sell her for me. He said it would be very difficult because of her club-foot. He suggested I went to see her vendor Ralph Fitzjohn and ask if he would take her back. I rushed up to him and I said, 'I've just bought your mare Mrs Moss and my husband's going to kill me. Would you take her back?' He looked at me quite calmly and said, 'You bought her. You keep her.'

I took her to Hollybush Green Stud, where we kept our mares at that time, but I didn't dare tell Robin about her and in fact hid her from him for a whole year. I did try to send her to Grundy, but I was told she was not good enough. How ironic that seems now. Buying Mrs Moss turned out to be inspired as she has become a legend in her own lifetime. Apart from my family, she is undoubtedly the best thing that has happened in my life.

She has produced ten individual winners and has four of her sons at stud. One is Precocious who was the undefeated winner of five races including the Gimcrack Stakes. He sadly cracked his knee and had to retire from racing as a two-year-old. Another is Krayyan standing in Ireland. The third is Jupiter Island, winner of the Japan Cup in Tokyo in 1986. He broke the track record and became the fastest British-bred horse ever over one and a half miles. He ran it in two minutes twenty-five seconds. The fourth son, Pandemonium, is at stud in New Zealand. But when I bought her, it didn't occur to me for a moment how magical and successful her future or the future of her children would be.

Although I initially felt very worried about my purchase, it didn't take long for Mrs Moss to prove herself. I sent her to be covered by Sharpen Up. The result was Socks Up, sold as a yearling in 1978 for £10,000. It was the first time we'd sold a yearling for a decent price. The following year, Mrs Moss had Pushy, also by Sharpen Up. We were going to sell her but when I went to see her just before the sales, Peter Diamond, the stud groom at the Overbury stud in Gloucestershire where Grundy was born, told me he thought she was a very nice filly and that I should try to keep her. Robin was very reluctant. In the end I persuaded him to agree by promising that if she was no good, I'd sell all our other horses. Andrew who was by now seventeen and as keen on horses as I was – he is now a partner in the Bloomsbury Stud and works for Tattersalls, the blood-stock auctioneers – suggested I send her to Henry Cecil to train. Henry agreed to take her and I drove her there myself in our box. When we arrived he called for someone to unload her and then stood with his head on one side and watched her walk away from him. He said, 'I'll win the Queen Mary for you with that.'

I'd always felt that if I had a two-year-old filly, the Queen Mary Stakes at Royal Ascot would be one of the races I would most want to win. And that one of the results would be a fantastic brood mare. I still feel the same and would be per-fectly content to have a brood mare band, all of them Queen Mary winners.

But I said to Henry, 'You don't have to do that much.' I didn't know at the time that he had never won the Queen Mary.

Pushy won her first two races and was entered to run at Ascot in the Queen Mary Stakes in 1980. There was a seventeen-runner field and a lot of very good fillies. The Aga Khan's filly Nasseem was favourite and, because they have bred con-sistently good horses since the beginning of this century, I thought that if Pushy managed to finish in front of Nasseem, she would have done really well. Joe Mercer was riding Pushy. I stood completely by myself on top of the stands. If I have a runner in a race I don't like to be with anybody. Before the race I felt very nervous and once it started I felt somehow disembodied as though it wasn't really happening. Pushy won by two lengths. I seemed to float totally dream-like and in slow motion down to the winners' enclosure. For weeks and weeks after that I used to wake up in the morning with a wonderful feeling of having achieved something very special. I don't think I've felt quite the same about any other race we've won, except perhaps the Japan Cup.

Pushy was the first of many successes. Since I bought Mrs Moss the Bedford family colours have won many races not only in England, but also in France, America and Japan. The children and grandchildren of Mrs Moss have won nearly £1 million in prize money. One of her granddaughters was sold in America for three-quarters of a million dollars and we turned down well over £1 million for Mrs Moss's son Precocious when he retired to stud in 1983. We've also been offered a lot of money for Mrs Moss, but I feel if I sold her, I wouldn't deserve anything in life again.

I don't really like selling any of the animals we breed. We originally sold Jupiter Island for £10,000, but bought him back five years later for £150,000.

Mrs Moss totally changed my life. She's the one thing that has happened only because of me. She has retired now. After fifteen foals I didn't think it would be fair to go on putting pressure on her foot. We've had her painted by Susan Crawford and in the summer of 1990 Philip Blacker, who used to be a National Hunt jockey, did a lifesize statue of her in bronze which stands in the park at Woburn.

The stud farm has been my biggest love. But I always had to steal time away from other things to be there. Robin always insisted that I had to take care of the children and deal with my responsibilities at Woburn first. Ironically it is now one of the last things I devote time to, which is sad. It is the biggest sacrifice that I have made since Robin's been ill.

We keep around sixty horses at Woburn. That is, brood mares and their followers – yearlings and foals. The numbers fluctuate depending on the time of year. We've got seventeen brood mares of our own and we look after some for other people too. Andrew and I and our wonderful stud groom Walter Wick do not run our stud conventionally. I feel that as horses are herd animals, they should be kept in groups so we don't keep them in boxes, but in yards. I don't believe horses thrive being kept on their own.

I try to refuse nearly all social engagements around foaling time as I hate not being there when the foals are born. Nearly all foals are born during the night, and all through the foaling season, someone sits up every night. We would never leave them to foal on their own. Nothing is more wonderful than seeing a mare foal and watching the foal get up, which nearly always happens within the first three-quarters of an hour. In fact, until it starts to race, you can learn more about a foal the night it's born than at any other time. That's when you see whether the little baby has got fight, drive and independence. Being born is its biggest effort until it has to run.

I think my years of learning to understand horses have been a marvellous training for understanding Robin after his stroke. A horse can only guide you about what it wants by its body language. Over the years I learned to tell if a horse felt fearful or content, anxious or peaceful, and I knew when it accepted and trusted me. Likewise before Robin could speak, I could see without his saying anything when he felt unhappy, apprehensive, or content. I have felt comfortable talking to horses. I never believed that there was no communication with a horse because it couldn't talk. Once I had got over the initial shock of Robin being unconscious, I could talk to him very easily.

The best preparation for coping with Robin's illness came about in 1983 after Mrs Moss had given birth to Putupon. She got an infection in her uterus and this resulted in a form of toxic shock which caused her to founder. She had developed serious laminitis in her club-foot. Laminitis is a very painful ailment that reduces the blood flow to the foot. In every case it causes severe pain and if it is not detected at once can be fatal.

Mrs Moss was in great distress. We thought at the time that the best treatment was to make her walk on the foot every couple of hours. The only way of getting her to do this was to take her foal away. I knew that because she was such a wonderful mother she would follow her. She did, struggling to her feet and following her foal round and round the big barn.

I've since discovered from a vet called Ric Redden, who is

one of the foot experts of the world, that my approach was not the correct way to deal with laminitis.

When horses are ill they very easily give up, so it was very important not to leave her alone. With the help of the stud groom we spent eleven days and nights with Mrs Moss, persuading her to walk every couple of hours, comforting her and encouraging her to live. I learned from the experience how important it is, when someone is ill, to put everything you can into giving them the will to live. Because Mrs Moss's illness went on for so long and was so exhausting, I became aware that in some ways when something terrible happens you can cope better when you are really tired. It helps blunt the emotions and you don't feel pain so acutely. That was why I didn't care how tired I got when Robin had his stroke. My feelings were partially numbed and that helped me cope. Those days and nights with Mrs Moss were a kind of training period.

Horses have also helped confirm my belief in the healing power of crystals. About four years ago I became interested in crystals and their special healing powers. I'm convinced that a horse that I thought was going to die recovered because of the crystal in my hand.

It happened on my birthday in 1988. We were in the middle of having lunch with lots of friends when Wally, our stud groom, rang and said that a foal had been badly kicked in the rib-cage by its mother. It had collapsed, was very distressed and its sides were heaving. He said it would take Brian Cox the vet thirty-five minutes to arrive. I abandoned my guests and rushed to be with it. When a horse is very distressed it often thrashes about, but if you put your knee on its neck it can't get up. I put my anorak down to protect its eye from the straw and waited for the vet to arrive. He gave it an intravenous saline drip and gently examined it. He said that there was a big dent in the rib-cage where three or four ribs had been pushed in, but that we wouldn't know until the following day what damage had been done to the spleen, kidneys, or liver. Fortunately its colour was good. You can tell from the inside of the eyes, nostrils and gums if a horse is haemorrhaging. I stayed in the stable for about three hours holding my crystal. Suddenly the telephone rang. There is quite a loud outside bell on the stud and as I jumped up to answer it, so did the foal. Then it shook itself. I couldn't believe it. It was carefully monitored for the next two weeks, but it never looked back. That must have had something to do with the crystal. I think there are times when something is so intense and you are so wrapped up in it that doubts, fears and embarrassment disappear and you give all your attention to what you are doing. I had a crystal with me all the time Robin was ill, and in fact keep one with me at all times.

I am a person who needs to be close to the earth. If I'm feeling confused and want to get back to normal as quickly as possible, it helps if I go and spend half an hour in the stable and turn the horses out or just muck out. I would find it hard to cope if I always stayed indoors, was formally dressed, lived the life some people think I should live and couldn't regularly touch the earth.

Chapter 7

Difficult Times

The secret of happiness is not in doing what one likes, but in liking what one does.   Sir James M Barrie

Henrietta

It was lucky that when we went to Woburn we'd already been married twelve years because we knew each other very well by then. We had a good working partnership in our marriage and that continued at Woburn. We shared a huge four-partner desk that my father-in-law bought for Woburn. It had belonged to Warren Hastings, founder of the East India Company. I'm very messy and Robin's very tidy, so his part was like the Sahara Desert and mine looked like a Soho market.

Robin would work in London on Tuesday, Wednesday and Thursday and come back to work at Woburn from Friday to Monday, so he had no rest at all. He made all the big policy decisions, and I did the day-to-day things. I tended to look after the catering, shops, house and antique centre, but if I ever did anything that he didn't approve of, it was always changed. I was really the personnel manager. People came to see me if they had any problems. If it was something I thought I could solve, I did so, otherwise I'd suggest they made an appointment with Robin. Although Robin never told me where my boundaries were, I felt I knew. For example, I would never have agreed to have a tree chopped down without asking him.

Robin would have all his meetings in our office and although I wasn't involved in everything, I overheard what was going on, listened to him talking on the telephone and learned a lot. I didn't know then how much this would help me when I had to take over after his stroke. Otherwise there would have been whole areas I would not have known anything about.

I learn quite quickly, which is partly due to my upbringing. I wasn't a girl to Daddy, I was a child with a brain and he always talked to me like an adult rather than a little girl and would often discuss business in front of me. I never heard him say something was beyond him or that he couldn't cope. I've never contemplated running away from things.

It was soon after we moved to Woburn that I took up doing tapestry. I spent a lot of the day listening and talking to people, but often nothing happened that would leave a mark. Robin would come back from London and ask me what I had done while he was away. I thought it would be a good idea to do tapestry so that if I had done eight square inches in a day, it was something tangible he could see. I have since taken my tapestry to meetings, done it on trains, in cars, while I'm talking on the telephone and particularly when I'm planning. It helps stop me being quite so impetuous.

However, from February until November while Robin was so ill, I did only one small cushion, which would normally have been a three-week project. I just couldn't do it. I suppose it's because I was very conscious that during those ten months there could be no planning.

Although I am strong-willed and have firm ideas of my own, I always went to Robin for advice. He was always at the end of the reins. I loved the feeling that I didn't have to pull on my own reins. He never let me be my own worst enemy. He made me feel totally safe. He would just give me a look or say, 'That's enough, Henrietta,' and it didn't matter whether we were at a dinner party, with great friends or at a trustee meeting. I always reacted positively.

We made several additions to Woburn. Paris House has become a wonderful restaurant backed by the Roux Brothers with their first English chef Peter Chandler. We created the Bloomsbury Stud and built two eighteen-hole championship golf courses.

When a house is open to the public it's a bit like the theatre – the show goes on regardless of problems. I remember one April morning in 1976 we discovered that the entire crypt was under water. A back-up pipe from the lake had become blocked and the water had pumped backwards into the house. We all went down there at 8.00 a.m. in our wellies and began to shovel water out. The house was due to open at 10.30 a.m. and it was a frantic rush. All the people who would normally sit in the rooms were downstairs helping us and we only just made it. It caused a lot of damage and the public couldn't go down there for days.

When you run a stately home, there is always a lot to be done. There must be sitters in all the rooms and guides to take people round. The rooms must be cleaned. We have a curator who is responsible for the collection, which includes paintings, furniture, porcelain, sculpture and silver. There are continual requests for different items to go on exhibition all over the world. There are experts who want to come and look at various objects. The house and the forty-acre garden have to be run. There's shooting, which means gamekeepers and pheasant-rearing. There's the antique centre. The estate comprises 13,000 acres, which includes 5,000 acres of woods, two championship golf courses and 3,500 acres farmed by us and the remainder let to tenants, all of which needs attention. We had just applied for planning permission for another golf course when Robin had his stroke. The park has 1,000 deer, including 400 Père David deer which originally came from China and were saved from extinction by the eleventh duke.

Following inquiries from the Chinese Government about the possibility of reintroducing the deer, Robin donated twenty-two Père David to the Chinese Government. They were taken to China by Andrew in 1985. Maya Boyd, a great friend of ours, whose late husband John was at Harvard with Robin, is an authority on the Père David deer and went to live in China to study them. When Robin had his stroke she came to see him at the National with all sorts of Chinese herbs and medicines for strokes. The doctors let him have some of them. There are 400 cottages on the estate and that requires a full maintenance programme. There's the stud which I manage day to day, but Robin and Andrew were always involved when I wanted to buy or sell an animal or plan the matings. We have been trying to redevelop the wild animal kingdom into a theme park. In fact we had just got to the crucial planning application stage when Robin had his stroke. Luckily we could go on because we knew Robin's thoughts. He felt it was vital to have something that would generate a big income to help us continue running and repairing the estate in the future. If we didn't, the estate might even have to be sold. Despite the thousands of visitors we get, Woburn loses approximately £500,000 a year. We need £400,000 a year for repairs alone.

The art collection, which includes works by Van Dyck, Reynolds, Gainsborough, Canaletto, Cuyp, Claude, Poussin and Murillo, must be worth countless millions, but we can't sell it. Or if we did we would have to give 87 per cent of the money realised to the government because as works of art they would no longer be exempted from estate duties.

If it wasn't for the Bedford estates in London which own property in Bloomsbury, Woburn would probably no longer exist as the family home.

I can think of houses much less grand than Woburn that are lived in much more lavishly. We don't have a very big staff now. There's Roger the butler, Paul the chef, Valerie, Julie and Cynthia who help run the house. There is also Mrs Whiteside who comes in daily; she used to look after us at Marquis Court.

We have four dailies for the public part of the house. When you consider the size of the house – there are about 90 rooms, 565 windows, 10 long corridors and 2 staircases – it's not very many people to do a big job.

I know people think how wonderful it must be to have a lot of money, because you can have everything you want, but it isn't that simple. We also have huge commitments and I have never just gone out and bought things without thinking. I won't fly first class because I think it is a terrible waste of money and I don't like spending a lot of money on clothes. Both of which help me feel less guilty about the money I spend on horses. Robin, however, would rather it was the other way round. He has always liked me to look elegant and has been so particular about my clothes that if I put on something he didn't feel was quite right for the occasion, he would make me change. My sons now do it to me too, and although it is annoying, I usually listen.

If you asked Robin what he dislikes most about me, he'd say he hates me looking a mess. He would prefer me to be very slim, nicely made up with my hair beautifully done all day long. I love dressing up for a party or to go racing, but if I am just going to be out on the estate or shopping, I don't see why I should look as if I have fallen out of *Vogue*.

I think the real value of money is in a crisis and the first time I realised it was in 1977 when Andrew had his nearly fatal car accident. Whatever doctor was needed, whatever anybody said should be done for him, we could do it. We didn't have to think whether we could afford it or whether the other children would be deprived.

Andrew was fifteen when it happened. He was a good all-round sportsman and enjoyed sport most at school. We'd just had the Neil Diamond concert at Woburn and he then left for the United States to stay with his godfather George Braga. He'd never been abroad on his own before, but I told myself that I couldn't keep him at my side for ever. Robin, Robbie, Jamie, Jamie's nanny and I went to see my parents in Spain. For the first five or six days that we were in Marbella, I had a terrible feeling that something awful was going to happen. Then on 11 August, the eighth day and the day before Robbie's birthday, the telephone rang at 3.00 a.m. It was Andrew's godfather to say that Andrew had had a car accident, was in intensive care and they didn't know how serious it was. It turned out that Andrew was being driven by his son Michael who had just passed his test.

We rushed to the airport. Robin discovered he didn't have

enough money on him to pay for the ticket to New York. We explained what had happened to people at the airport and they allowed him to get on a plane, leaving me as surety until the money was telexed through. I'm sure only a Latin country would do something like that. As we sat waiting for the plane to take off I said to Robin, 'Now whatever you do, if you're not happy with the doctor, change him.' Daddy had always impressed upon me that I must never be intimidated by doctors, because, depending on the area they were dealing with, a doctor is really a plumber or an electrician of the body, and that if one wasn't happy with one plumber or electrician, one should find another.

Daddy's attitude had a lasting effect on me that not only influenced Andrew's care but later Robin's when he had his stroke.

Andrew had blood clots everywhere and nearly died. His pelvis was broken in seventeen places and his hip socket in four, but luckily there was no brain damage. He needed several operations, which couldn't be done in the hospital he was in. Robin had to make the decision whether or not to move him. Because of the innumerable blood clots, it was a particularly difficult decision to make. Robin decided he had to be moved and Andrew survived. In a way it was a trial run for the decisions Andrew had to make over his father. I stayed with our other children and didn't go to America until nearly the end of August. The two weeks that Andrew and his father spent together made an incredible bond between them. I am sure that it was only because Andrew had been so ill himself that he had the courage to make the life-or-death decision to move his father from Milton Keynes to the National Hospital in Queen Square.

During the early days of Robin's illness, Andrew kept saying how wonderful it was to be able to repay a debt in almost the same way.

From the end of August Robin had to keep going back to London to work, Robbie went back to board at Harrow and I stayed with Andrew in America until just before Christmas. Jamie came out twice with his nanny and although he was only two, he remembers seeing Andrew in hospital.

Although once I had seen Robin after he had had his stroke I never doubted his survival, I didn't have the same instinct about Andrew. There was something terribly sad about someone very young being damaged and I didn't know for a long time whether or not he would be all right.

He had a major operation three weeks after his accident. It took over nine hours and we were told he ran a 25 per cent chance of dying during the operation if a blood clot went to either his heart or brain. It was the longest day we've ever spent. We all learned from the experience that when someone is seriously ill, that is all that counts and you put everything into helping that person recover. I learned that you can drop everything, that things will get done if you have a good team, as long as the team considers that what you're doing is more important than what you would normally be doing. Crises raise people to their highest level. Nobody wants to let anybody down. A lot of people say to me now, 'You weren't in your office for months, when Robin was ill and Woburn ran well, why don't you go away for a long holiday now?' But if I said I wanted to go to Tahiti and lie on a beach for months, people wouldn't pull their weight in the same way.

Andrew was in hospital from 12 August until the middle of October. We were then advised to take him somewhere warm so he could convalesce. We went to California, but unfortunately he developed an infection due to the screw plates in his hip so within a few days he was back in hospital and stayed there until Christmas.

He had massive doses of antibiotics by intravenous infusion for three months, which meant if he got ill with an infection that needed to be treated with antibiotics they wouldn't have worked so well.

When I came back with Andrew from America Robin had organised a wonderful surprise for me. The flag flying over Woburn which until then had the Bedford crest on it, was now intertwined with my family crest. It still flies over the house today.

Andrew was then on crutches for two years and we had to

change his school. He had been at Harrow but as all the classes took place in different buildings, it was impossible for him both to carry his books and walk. He went to a crammer in Worcester called St Cloud. Robbie felt that it was unfair that Andrew was having a different education from him and wanted to go too. Although it was not a school we would have picked when we had the choice of all the top public schools, we let him go.

Even now Andrew's hip is all pieced together. He can't ride a horse, play games, dance or do the sort of things that young men of his age like to do.

One day he'll be whole again, because he will be able to have an artificial hip. But they won't do it yet for two reasons: one because for twenty years after you have a bone infection you are at risk of it starting up again if you have a fall or cut through it; also because if you put an artificial hip into someone so young, it won't last his lifetime.

We went through a very tricky time when he was determined to find a doctor who would replace his hip earlier. He said he didn't want to dance when he was sixty. He wanted to dance now. It has been very hard for him to walk with a stick because he was so active and sports-orientated and it's been difficult for him socially.

In spite of all this, he now says it was the best thing that ever happened to him, because he appreciates so many things that he might not otherwise have done. He ceased to be a child after his accident. He no longer treated us as his parents. We became his friends.

The other trauma in my life occurred when I felt I was losing Robin's love. Because we had married as children, we probably should have sat down every five or six years and worked out where we had got to in our marriage, and grown up together, but we didn't. I felt at the time that there was a distinct possibility that Robin would leave me and for the first time looked at our marriage in the round. I remember saying to myself, 'Is it pride because you've lost face or do you really love him?' I realised I couldn't live without him. I had no feeling of pride at all. I didn't mind what I did as long

as he didn't leave me. Our marriage was much stronger afterwards. It made me grow up.

In 1986 Robin and I celebrated our silver wedding anniver-
sary. We had a lovely dinner party at Harry's Bar surrounded by friends. Robin gives most generous presents, but
I was desperate trying to think what to give him. I felt it had
to be something imaginative. I finally decided to give him a
silver plate for each year of our marriage, with an appropriate quotation to that year. I have always noted down in
the back of my diary quotations or particular comments that
I have liked. I had a small coat of arms engraved at the top
of the plate and the relevant year engraved on the bottom. I
have added to the collection every year ever since.

Robin was very uncommunicative during the last year
before he had his stroke. In fact he had become so withdrawn
and difficult, that I'd almost got to the point where I
couldn't cope. It wasn't that I didn't love him any more. I
couldn't cope because he never talked to me. I knew he was
having terrible headaches, but he kept saying he didn't have
time to go to the doctor. The awful thing is that his stroke
could have been avoided. I noticed that when he had a headache his eye went out of sync and that his pupil dilated.

If I had just explained that to a doctor he would have done
an angiogram, a brain scan that looks at the blood vessels in
the brain, and seen that he had an aneurism, a weakness in a
blood vessel.

He would have had an operation. It would have been
difficult to clip the aneurism because of its size, but if it
had been done, he never would have had a stroke, never lost
consciousness, nor had nearly his entire brain flooded with
blood. The whole thing could have been avoided. Had I had
a horse that exhibited clinical signs like that, I'm sure I would
have talked to the vet about it. But because Robin never
really talked about his headaches to me, it never occurred
to me to do anything about it for him. It was terrible
negligence.

Robin was also very busy that year. In addition to his work
in the City and running Woburn, he was planning a campaign

to raise money for the Kennedy Memorial Trust. He felt very honoured that he was asked to be its chairman – a five-year appointment – as the chairman is chosen by the Prime Minister and the American President. The trust was founded by Lord Harlech in memory of his great friend President Kennedy and when Lord Harlech died Robin was picked to replace him. It's a very generous scholarship for university graduates, to go to Harvard, the Massachusetts Institute of Technology, or the Kennedy School of Government, and be Kennedy scholars for a year of postgraduate studies.

There were twelve students a year selected not only for their ability, but also for their aims and personality. The trustees wanted to increase the number of students to about sixteen and Robin was working very hard before his stroke on planning how to fund-raise £1 million. He had made a list of organisations and individuals to approach and while he was so ill Andrew went to see everyone Robin had on his list. He was determined to get the money raised for his father.

For someone of twenty-six who really has never had to do anything like that, it was a very plucky thing to do.

In the end he raised over £600,000. Mrs Thatcher gave a dinner at Downing Street for all the major benefactors in July 1989. Robin was by then well enough to attend and stood up and made a very brief speech. It was very touching because in Mrs Thatcher's reply she paid tribute to his courage.

I remember the Christmas before Robin's stroke he said he wanted a labrador that would be a gun dog. We were told the name of an excellent breeder and she came over with five four-month-old puppies for us to see so that Robin could choose one. He saw one he really loved. The puppy seemed quite shy, but kept coming up to Robin. We called her China because her mother was called Tasse De Thé. China was with Robin when he had his stroke.

Robin became increasingly difficult to make contact with during the few months that led up to his stroke. He was aloof, removed, withdrawn and often angry. He wasn't just like that with me. He was the same with the children and the people who work at Woburn.

The aneurism was probably already seeping, but I didn't know at the time that his behaviour was because he was ill. It must have been particularly difficult for him to concentrate during the last few weeks.

The way he left all his papers, he must have thought he was going to die. He has always been a very organised person and kept every subject on his desk in different piles, but when his secretary Cilla Pumfrey came in on Monday morning, the day after his stroke, his desk was in total confusion. She said he must have had the most terrible morning before his stroke because he was quite obviously unable to separate things. But amongst the chaos there were instructions on what to do about everything. Robin doesn't remember a thing about it. His long-term memory has been wiped out from December 1987 two months before his stroke, until the middle of August 1988. It's a complete void.

The Thursday evening before his stroke we went to a dinner party given by Gerald and Gail Ronson. There were about fourteen of us altogether. I was sitting next to Gerald and Robin sat across the table from me next to Gail on one side and Sylvia Leigh on the other. I noticed Robin seemed to be having a very animated conversation with Sylvia. After dinner Gail took me to one side and said, 'It's extraordinary. Five or six years ago Sylvia had the most horrendous stroke, the doctors didn't think she would live and when she did that she would never speak again.'

I watched her very carefully after that. You couldn't have known that anything like that had happened to her. She wrote to me as soon as she heard about Robin's stroke saying, 'Never give up. It's thanks to my husband's dedication to me that I am now perfectly all right, but it can take a long, long time.' She offered to do anything she could.

I'm sure seeing her with my own eyes probably gave me the arrogance to believe that Robin would be perfectly all right after his stroke. It convinced me that such a recovery was possible. Something I might not have felt otherwise.

After the dinner party we both went back to Clarendon Place. I was supposed to go to my desperately ill mother the next day. I went out to a meeting in the morning and came back with the most appalling headache. I lay down on the bed and Robin said to me, 'You shouldn't fly with such a headache. Perhaps you should postpone your trip.' I was absolutely torn. In retrospect I feel that perhaps I was meant to stay here. But at the time I felt I had to go to Mummy. I said to Robin, 'What about the terrible headaches you get?' And he said, 'That's different. Don't worry about me.'

Chapter 8

The Stroke and its Aftermath

All glory comes from daring to begin.   Eugene F Ware

A stroke is to the brain what a coronary thrombosis is to the heart and the brain will be damaged by a stroke just as the heart is damaged by a 'coronary'.

Each year about 100,000 people suffer from a stroke in England and Wales and about 28 per cent of strokes are fatal. It is the third highest cause of death after cancer and heart attacks.

At least half of all strokes are caused by high blood pressure. Other major contributory factors are smoking, drinking, unhealthy diets and the contraceptive pill.

All strokes vary enormously in severity and symptoms, but there are two main types. One is caused when a blood clot forms and blocks the flow of blood to part of the brain. The other, when a damaged blood vessel bursts and blood pours into the brain. This second type is known as a brain haemorrhage or sub-arachnoid haemorrhage. The commonest cause of a haemorrhage is an aneurism, a weak spot in an artery that makes it liable to rupture.

Strokes caused by blood clots are more common, usually occur in older people and account for about 8 per cent of deaths.

Strokes caused by haemorrhages usually occur in younger people and kill about 20 per cent of sufferers. It was this type of stroke that nearly killed Robin Tavistock.

Some people are born with an aneurism, but if it doesn't rupture, they can go through life never knowing they have it. A stroke caused by an aneurism happens quite suddenly. The blood vessel literally falls apart, blood leaks into the brain and if it is a big leak, the person will die immediately. Statistics show that four out of ten people who have a brain haemorrhage don't survive the initial bleed.

The symptoms of the remaining six vary enormously from a severe headache to, as in the case of Lord Tavistock, deep unconsciousness. Unfortunately the prognosis for these six is not good. Half of them will suffer from a further bleed and will almost certainly die. Their chances are improved, however, if they can be operated on after the first bleed to remove the pool of blood from the head, relieve the pressure and prevent the leaking spot from a further fatal bleed.

The blood pouring into the brain causes considerable damage. The brain itself has the consistency of soft margarine and when there is a haemorrhage it has a similar effect to squirting a garden hose at high pressure into margarine. When the damage is severe, permanent paralysis may result. Depending on the area of the brain involved and how much of it has been damaged, the stroke can cause weakness, paralysis of the arm and leg on either the left or right side of the body and twisting of the face. Speech, hearing, control of bladder and bowels, understanding and concentration can also be affected. All the symptoms of a stroke are caused by brain damage. The brain cells which were badly damaged when the stroke occurred die and never recover. Other cells which were only partially damaged, due to swelling of the brain, recover and start working again, usually during the first few weeks after the stroke.

When Robin arrived at the National Hospital, he was immediately taken up into the Intensive Care Unit. He was put on to a respirator to help him breathe and his responses were tested.

'His neurological observations were very bad,' Sister Queally remembered. 'We asked him to squeeze a hand, but he did not respond. We then tested his reaction to pain. Someone who is conscious or lightly unconscious automatically moves their arm or leg away from the pain. Robin, however, did not. Instead he moved his hands and feet away from his body in an outward curving movement.

'This is recognised as a very bad neurological sign and means there is considerable pressure building up in the head. Such pressure causes brain damage which is often irrevocable. We also tested the reaction of his pupils. They did not react at all to light. It was a very bad sign.'

The prognosis was very poor. Robin was given a brain scan. This shows in three dimensions exactly where a haemorrhage has occurred, whether it is in a part of the brain that is operable, and how much damage has already been caused. The scan revealed that Robin had a giant aneurism of 2.5 cm by 3.5 cm on the carotid artery beside the left optic nerve which had ruptured extensively. Surgery to drain the blood from the brain and clip the aneurism so that it didn't bleed again was the important next step. However, medical opinion is divided between those who feel that it is better to wait before operating until the brain begins to heal itself and the patient regains consciousness, and those who prefer to operate quickly.

Robin was examined by a surgeon, Mr David Thomas, who spoke to Andrew and was waiting to speak to Henrietta when she arrived. He felt it was better to wait before operating until Robin had recovered from the initial devastating effects of his stroke and he recommended to the family that they wait about ten days. Henrietta and Andrew felt instinctively uneasy and asked for a second opinion.

Henrietta remembered that a year previously when the Aga Khan's son Hussein had suffered severe head injuries in a water skiing accident, the Aga Khan had asked Robin to help him find a top brain surgeon. She rang the Aga Khan and asked him the name of the doctor and if he could contact him.

The surgeon concerned was Alan Crockard. By a lucky coincidence he also operated at the National Hospital. Henrietta asked if he could come and examine her husband.

By this time details of Lord Tavistock's illness had been broadcast on the news. Flowers began arriving at the hospital and the telephones at the National Hospital, Woburn and Clarendon Place rang continuously.

Henrietta and the rest of the family stayed at the hospital most of the night but eventually returned to Clarendon Place at 4.00 a.m.

Henrietta told Jamie to get to bed quickly, 'But,' she said, 'a few minutes later he came into my bedroom, went round to Robin's side of the bed and said, "If you don't mind Mummy, I will be sleeping here until Daddy comes home." And he did.'

'I felt,' said Jamie, 'that it was my turn to be strong for Mummy. Once Daddy had arrived at the National, I felt strongly that he wouldn't die.'

Henrietta lay down on the bed, 'But,' she says, 'I don't think I went to sleep.'

What kept running through my head during those two hours was what my father told me about doctors being like plumbers and electricians and that if one wasn't happy with one plumber or electrician one should find another. I remembered how Robin and I discussed it before he flew to America after Andrew had his terrible accident.

Now I had seen Robin, I didn't think he would die. I felt inside that he was going to be perfectly all right but my feelings were so alien to what I was being told that I couldn't tell them to anybody. I would have sounded uncaring and arrogant. I was back at the hospital by about 6.00 a.m. and soon afterwards Chuck Downer arrived. When Andrew had spoken to him the night before he'd had under two hours to catch the last flight from Boston to London, but he'd made it.

'No matter what I had on, I was going to see Robin in London,' explained Chuck. 'I think of Robin as the brother I never had. There was no question in my mind about it. Andrew telephoned me at 4.00 p.m. Boston time. I had been out all day and walked in the door as the phone was ringing. It was so lucky he got me. Andrew was crying and told me it was touch and go and his father might not last the night. I was praying that he would hold on until I got to him. I had this feeling that if I could talk to him, I could get him to hold on.'

When Chuck arrived, he went straight in to see Robin, gave him an enormous hug and then asked the nurse if he could shave him. 'I wanted to be close to him, shave him, wipe his brow, hold his hand, anything,' he said. 'You don't realise how important someone is to you until something like that happens. I had always considered him as my best friend. He was always there. Now there was this terrible shock that he might not be there in half an hour. I took every chance I had to be close to him.'

At 8.30 a.m. Mr Thomas telephoned Mr Crockard and asked if he would come over to the Intensive Care Unit and give the requested second opinion.

Also early that morning an angiogram was performed. Dye was injected into the brain's arteries to give a clear picture of exactly where the leaking artery was. 'I was told that the area was very difficult to get to,' said Henrietta, 'and in order to reach it they had to cut through an unaffected but very important part of the brain. There was the worry that an operation might not be possible because in order to get to the affected part, so much damage to other areas of the brain would be done that it wouldn't be worth it.'

Later that day Alan Crockard arrived to examine Robin and study the brain scan and angiogram.

'It was obvious,' he said, 'that he had had a devastating brain haemorrhage and that his brain was very sick. If he had not been on a ventilator and all the other equipment he would certainly have died. When you get to the stage that the pupils do not react, it means the brain is in a very poor condition. We grade stroke comas. Robin was in a grade four coma which is the deepest. The prognosis was pretty bad. Added to that were the technical hazards of the procedure because a giant aneurism is very difficult to clip. I thought he had less than a 10 per cent chance of survival.

'However, once you had accepted that the chances of his survival were very poor, you either left the situation as it was, or you said, "It's very bad and it can't really get very much worse, so let's operate and do what we can." I felt that the very large aneurism would bleed again. It was obvious that his condition was not only due to the injury that the brain had had as a result of the initial haemorrhage, but to a blood clot that the scan revealed inside his head. If we got the clot out, I believed he might actually improve.

'What I didn't know was to what extent the blood vessel bursting had already irreparably damaged his brain. I realised the chances of successful surgery were limited. Even if I removed the clot and relieved the pressure in the brain by getting out the pool of blood, the aneurism might leak again. It is also impossible to predict if a complication will occur when you try to clip the aneurism. I also had to consider that when someone is as sick as Robin was, the brain doesn't actually tolerate a major operation very well. This is one reason why there are those who prefer to wait for a few weeks for the brain to partially heal itself, which will make it better able to cope with an operation.

'However, I belong to the school that says, "Things are bad, but the clot itself may be making it worse. If we can get the clot out, we'll have helped the brain. If we seal the blood vessel, we can start a more aggressive regime aimed at brain recovery. Let's go early."

'I have spent some time working in Belfast where I was faced with horrendous and devastating injuries, when split-second decisions had to be made, and this experience helped me to make up my mind. It was a complex decision based on instinct as well as experience. I had to weigh everything up, do a balancing act and come up with a decision. One can compare it to people making decisions over buying and selling currencies, or which horse is going to win the Derby. But for surgeons like myself the decision involves people's lives.

'I gave the family the background and my opinion. While I felt there was a valid point for waiting and seeing how things would go, I felt that things were so bad that Robin had very little to lose if things went wrong.

'The family were faced with two options: waiting for his general condition to improve before he had an operation, hoping that in the meantime the aneurism wouldn't bleed again, or going ahead with an early operation which might not be successful.'

It was an agonising choice, but one which the family reached quite quickly.

Henrietta
From the moment I saw Alan Crockard I felt totally confident. We decided to let Robin be operated on as soon as possible. I relied on my instinct throughout Robin's illness, even when people tried to persuade me I was doing the wrong thing. Two years before Robin's stroke Morgan Wheelock, who has been a friend since Robin's time at Harvard, said something to me that I've remembered ever since. It was that if I ever had a problem in my life, I should never over-think it. That my instinct would be my best ally and I should always follow it. I'd always felt I was instinctive, but there were times

when I'd stop myself and question whether I was doing the right thing.

He was the first person who gave me confidence in my instinct and from then on I had more confidence in doing things the way I do.

My father always told me that I had two spirit guides, which are not God, but people who have lived before. He used to say that one was more capable than the other and when I felt everything was going well, it was because both of them were there. I see one of them as the thinker and the other as the one who makes sure that the ends get tidied up, and when I'm left only with the one who tidies up, I don't operate so well. Both of them stayed with me all the time Robin was ill. Knowing as little as I knew about the brain and anything to do with neurology, when I look back now, the intuitive understanding I had of the problems and what to do, could not have been anything to do with me. It must have been my spirit guides.

They told Alan Crockard of their decision. Robin, however, wasn't well enough to have the operation on the Monday.

One of the family or his friends sat with him and talked to him round the clock. It was usually a member of the family during the day and Lynda Berry and Chuck Downer used to do the nights.

'I stayed with Robin every night for ten days,' said Chuck. 'I didn't want to leave his side.'

Henrietta encouraged everyone to talk to her husband.

I remembered reading that one of the most important things to help reawaken someone who is unconscious is smell and sound. I made a list of all Robin's favourite songs and our friend David Jacobs made a tape of them. He put Neil Diamond's 'Beautiful Noise', which is Robin's particular favourite, on every third track and we played it to him regularly.

Robin is the sort of man who never looks messy and I knew that he liked the smell of a certain kind of soap called 'Fleurs des Alpes'. I knew you could get it at Annabel's so later on Monday I asked Roger to go to Annabel's, explain he was Lord Tavistock's butler and ask if they would give him some soap.

Roger felt very embarrassed. 'Because I always worked at Woburn, I didn't know London at all. I asked Roy the chauffeur to drive me. I'd hardly walked down the first step when the doorman asked me what I wanted. I said, "This is going to sound very strange, but you must know Lord Tavistock?" He said he did. So I said, "I don't know if you know, but he's very seriously ill in hospital and they want to give him a bed-bath and they want to use his favourite soap, "Fleurs des Alpes", which is in your washrooms." He told me to wait and eventually came back up with three tablets in a box. The doorman must have told Mark Birley, the owner of Annabel's, because the next day "Fleurs des Alpes" soap, talcum powder and everything was delivered to the hospital.'

Monday was a very long day of waiting and hoping. A steady stream of visitors arrived at the hospital.

'I don't know whether it was a good or bad thing to do but as soon as people came we took them in to see Daddy,' said Andrew. 'We never hid him from anybody. To start with everyone was horrified by the number of tubes running in and out of everywhere. The sheer number of machines and gadgets and flashing digital displays was very off-putting. We learned to warn people what to expect. We told them to ignore all the machines and just go up to Daddy, hold his hand and talk to him.'

Morgan Wheelock who arrived from America to visit Robin admits he initially found the experience terrifying. 'It was the first time I had ever seen anyone in such a state,' he said. 'I found it so shocking partly because I identified with the situation so much that I feared for myself.' Andrew, however, wasn't put off. 'I didn't find the machines frightening because I'd been in hospital myself and also dealt with sick animals. I thought my father looked much younger, far less strained and as if he was just asleep.'

Andrew's ability to cope impressed Robbie. 'He was as calm as can be, dealing with everything and telling everybody what to do. He takes after my mother who is very good at taking control in a situation like that. They are both very logical. I don't know if I agree with their logic all the time, but in this case they took charge extremely well.'

Henrietta was delighted to be able to rely on Andrew. 'I was in control initially, but after three or four days Andrew took over. He was the main organiser and planner.'

Andrew was pleased to be able to do so much. 'I felt it was an opportunity for me to repay some of the things my father had done for me when I was ill. One very rarely gets the chance to say thank you to one's parents, or show them how much you love them or how much you care.'

By the end of that first day, Robin began to show a slight improvement. His pupils were beginning to react to light and his limbs moved slightly.

Henrietta went home, but couldn't sleep.

Then I remembered reading that during the Falklands War the pilots had taken some amazing pills so they could sleep deeply but only for a short time. I asked my GP for them the next day. They were called Temazepam and Andrew, Robbie, Jamie and I all took them. They were wonderful because we fell asleep quickly and woke up five hours later feeling brand-new.

On Tuesday Robin maintained his slight improvement. His father the Duke of Bedford arrived with his wife Nicole. He looked very tearful.

When Ian arrived back from skiing on the Sunday night that Robin had his stroke, Nicole told him that I had rung to say that Robin wasn't very well and although it was nothing serious, maybe it would be a good idea if she booked a plane and they came to London. However Robin's half-brother Francis rang and told Ian that Robin was in intensive care so he arrived feeling very upset. I had hoped that I would be able to lean on him, but it was quickly apparent that I wouldn't be able to.

He went in to see his son, but found the experience very traumatic. 'When Grandpa came,' said Jamie, 'he just couldn't hold Daddy's hand and talk to him.'

At 5.00 p.m. on Tuesday Robin had another brain scan and Alan Crockard made the decision to proceed with surgery the following day.

That night, however, the buzzers on Lord Tavistock's life support machines went off and the machines stopped working. Nurses came running from all directions. A fuse had gone in one of the machines. All the pipes were whipped out of Robin, and he was wheeled speedily across the ward and plugged in to another set of machines on the other side. The patient seemed none the worse for the experience.

The following morning, Wednesday 24 February, Robin was visited by Alan Crockard at 9.00 a.m. and pronounced well enough for surgery later that day.

Henrietta

I can now hardly believe that from the Sunday night to the Wednesday when Robin had his operation was only two whole days. It now seems the longest part of his whole recovery.

Constantly in my mind on that Wednesday morning was a promise Robin and I made to each other once, after we had seen a film about someone in a coma. It was that neither of us would let the other be left long-term on a life support machine. I told Alan Crockard that Robin wouldn't want to live and be paralysed. He told me that he understood. I felt confident that if he'd opened up the head and thought Robin could only live as a vegetable, he wouldn't have lived.

Alan Crockard in turn warned the family that as the aneurism was pressing on the optic nerve, even if Lord Tavistock came through the operation, he might be blind in one eye.

Andrew wanted to stay with his father until the last possible moment. His father had always stayed with him every time he had been operated on after his accident. He went up in the lift with him to the operating theatre on the sixth floor. 'Just outside the lift is a red line and I was asked not to come any further,' he said. 'Alan Crockard was there and said to me, "I will do everything I can for him, but if I feel that nothing can be done, I won't try." I broke down in tears and then spent the hours while he was in surgery pacing up and down in the hospital and round and round in the square outside.'

Chuck Downer managed to find an empty room in the hospital and had a good cry. 'So much emotion had built up. I spent an hour in that room repeating and repeating the words, "Hold on, Robin. Hold on." I also thought about how much Robin meant to me, what a good and loyal friend he'd been and what a loss I'd feel if he didn't make it.'

Henrietta found she couldn't stay in the hospital at all.

Whenever the children had operations I've always wanted to stay, yet that day I just couldn't. Ten minutes before the operation when I was about to leave there was a telephone call for me. It was Dr Robert Runcie, the Archbishop of Canterbury, calling from Australia. He said, 'I'm standing on my head and praying for him.'

She decided instead to go to St Clement Danes church, which was nearby.

It has always had special significance for me because it is where we were married and where Robbie was christened. I thought: If I go and sit in the church, somehow I'd know what was happening.

I didn't want to tell anyone, but I realised it would be very selfish of me to disappear. If the worst did happen, no one would know where I was and everyone would be put through extra trauma trying to find me. So I rang Jeni Sieff, who I knew was going to be at the hospital, and told her. But I didn't tell anyone else, not even Andrew.

Good team work is essential for a major operation like Lord Tavistock's. Assisting Mr Crockard was Mr Ianotti. The anaesthetics were handled by Dr Hirsch and Dr Calder.

'It's important to get the brain in the best possible state for an operation like the one performed on Robin,' explained Alan Crockard. 'Dr Calder did everything to get the brain in the best nutritional condition and then before the actual surgery produced a barbiturate coma which literally puts the brain to sleep for a long time and also protects the brain. Robin was kept on a ventilator.'

Alan Crockard admits it was a very difficult operation. The blood vessel that had leaked was the carotid artery, which is one of the main blood vessels going to the brain. It was on the left side and, in a right-handed person like Robin, the left side of the brain is the dominant one controlling speech, arm and leg movements and intellectual abilities.

'It was in a very difficult place to get to,' admits Crockard, 'and if in the course of the operation this blood vessel had been damaged, Robin could have woken up as a vegetable. He could also have ended up a vegetable if the operation didn't go very well. He might also have been a vegetable already as a result of the haemorrhage.

'However, the fact that there were some signs of improvement between Sunday and Wednesday helped confirm my belief that getting the clot out of his head and preventing the aneurism from leaking again, would leave him the best possible chance of recovery. The aneurism was large and pressing on the optic nerve to Robin's left eye and almost certainly accounted for the severe headaches he had suffered from for years. In fact looking into his eye, it was obvious that there had been pressure on that nerve for some time by the aneurism.

'The haemorrhage could have been avoided if he had had a brain scan earlier, but when you reckon that aneurisms are of the order of one in ten thousand of us, do we give everybody who has a pain behind the eye a brain scan? Everything in life is easy in retrospect.

'To get at the aneurism we actually had to stop the flow in the carotid blood vessel for a few minutes. This meant we made an incision in his neck and found the blood vessel below the aneurism, so that once everything was prepared, we could stop the blood above and below the aneurism and also incidentally to some of his dominant hemisphere. We made an incision on the temple behind the hairline, made a few drill-holes in the bone, lifted off a small segment of the bone, opened the coverings of the brain and then gently supported the brain, between the base of the skull and the undersurface of the brain. It was vital not to put a lot of pressure on the brain and amongst other things I used an operating microscope.

'Then having prepared everything and stopped the circulation for some time I went ahead. I needed about six or seven minutes to get the clot out, relieve the pressure, identify the aneurism, find its relation to the optic nerve, manipulate the blood vessel to get hold of the aneurism and put a special spring clip over it to stop it leaking again.

'There was a real chance that we might have to divide the optic nerve to the left eye to reach it, but fortunately we didn't. There was also a chance that I would not be able to control the aneurism and that it would continue to bleed. Robin's brain might not have been able to tolerate the temporary shut-off of the blood supply, in which case he might have died during or shortly after the operation.

'But I was dealing with a situation where his chances of surviving, in the state he was in, were two out of ten. How much worse can you get? When you're functioning at that level, if there's a chance I felt it was all to go for.

'The operation took about four hours. When you actually operate you have been trained to forget about the person and concentrate on the specific bits of the body: an aneurism, a blood vessel, a brain. It is only when you see the person once the protective towels are taken off again, that the patient becomes "human" again.

'The operation seemed to have gone well. The clot was removed, the leaking point dealt with, and the patient seemed to have tolerated the operation well. I couldn't, however, at that stage make any guess as to how good his recovery would be. In crude terms, for a surgeon, an operation is a success if the patient doesn't die on the table. But if the patient is left as a vegetable, as far as the family is concerned, it has been a failure.

'It is important to realise that when an event like this has occurred, the whole family is going through a major trauma. If one regards oneself only as the person wielding the surgical instrument, then that's only being a technician. Looking after and discussing the situation with the family, although less dramatic is every bit as important.

'Andrew, as well as coping with an ill father, also suddenly had to cope with all the responsibilities of the family thrust on to him. There were the worries of Robin's father, the Duke of Bedford. It's very hard for a man in great health to see his son struck down in front of him. And of course there are the anxieties of the wife. Social standing doesn't make any difference. All families have similar problems.'

After the operation Lord Tavistock was returned to the Intensive Care Unit and his barbiturate coma continued.

'We infused his brain with a drug called thiopentone,' said Dr

Hirsch, 'which actually rests the brain. We did an electro-encephalogram – an EEG – and I infused just enough drug to produce a flat EEG which means there was no activity in the brain at all. The metabolism of the brain is reduced which enables it to rest and helps it recover. He was kept on a breathing machine.'

*　　*　　*

Henrietta
When I reached the church I walked down the wide aisle and sat for a long time in the very last pew on the left-hand side. I went all through our marriage vows and thought about our life together. I thought about what Robin and I went through during the long nine hours of Andrew's operation. It made me feel a little easier. I thought about the good and the bad in our lives and made peace between us. I suppose I was preparing myself in case he died.

I walked slowly round the church and read all the inscriptions and memorials to the brave pilots who gave their lives to help Britain win the war. Then I went down to the crypt where Robbie was christened. The altar is made out of granite and quite plain.

I stayed there for what must have been hours, until I finally went back to the hospital. As I was leaving I noticed a sandwich-board outside the church which said 'Communion every day at noon'. I thought: If the operation has been successful and Robin seems all right, I'll come in the morning and sit through the service. But as I had not been confirmed, I wouldn't take Communion.

I walked back. There were friends sitting in the waiting-room of the Intensive Care Unit. I saw Andrew walking down the corridor towards me. He gave me an enormous hug and said he'd been worried about me and that someone had just come to say that the operation was nearly over and had gone well so far.

Less than an hour later Alan Crockard came down and explained everything that he'd done. He took us all into a room, pulled Jamie against him and held him tight while he talked. Apparently when he opened Robin's head the pressure was such that he didn't think he would last another twenty-four hours. He said he'd put three clips on the aneurism because it was so big and explained that Robin had been put into a barbiturate coma to give his brain more chance to rest and that he had not needed to cut the optic nerve so there was a chance his sight would return.

That night about ten of us, all the family and a few friends, went out to Harry's Bar for dinner. I think if I'd been sitting in that restaurant and seen us all walk in, I would have been deeply shocked. We all thought afterwards: How did we get there? But at the time it seemed fine.

We felt such relief that the operation was over and that Robin was alive.

I remember when the waiter came to take our order Charles Chelsea said, 'The one thing I don't think I'll be eating this evening is brains.' We all roared with laughter. It sounds terrible but at the time it didn't seem to be. We had a camaraderie that was quite extraordinary. People laughed like they never laughed before. It was a bit like the war. I don't know why we did it. The memory of it is wonderful, but the concept is almost obscene.

Chapter 9

The Slow Route Back

If you never imagine miracles, they will never happen.
Sir Colin Coote

Robin was kept in a barbiturate coma for two or three days after the operation. It was a difficult time for friends and family as his life hung in the balance. There was a strong possibility that he would not regain consciousness.

Henrietta
Alan Crockard didn't offer a prognosis, and I never asked for one. I felt it was pointless. He could obviously give me statistics on what usually happened, but how could he tell me exactly what was going to happen to Robin?

I knew that after the operation there would be a lot of bruising and fluid in the brain and that it would be impossible to work out which parts of the brain had been only temporarily damaged by the bruising and which parts had been permanently damaged by the haemorrhage. I just instinctively felt that he would be all right. Although it was a terrible thing to have happened, I somehow did not feel depressed. I suppose it was because I was surrounded by so many people who gave me so much support.

Although I maintained my sense of confidence in my husband's recovery, many others including doctors, relatives and friends were not so confident.

Many people said he'd never come round after the operation

or that if he did come out of the coma, he'd never walk again or be an imbecile. It was hard to cope with and sometimes got me down. But most of the time I forced negative thoughts out of my head and tried to think positively throughout. I felt so strongly about the power of positive thinking that I didn't want anyone to be around him who thought he was going to die. I only wanted people who knew he was going to live.

Andrew agreed. 'Sometimes we had to be quite hard with people. Everyone who was going to see Daddy whether it was for thirty seconds or half an hour had to go in strong and relay strength to him.

'We wanted them to speak to him normally. If they felt frightened or tearful, we asked them to leave the room immediately. We didn't want anything negative. I think people understood after a while.'

Henrietta

What Robin needed to know most was that people loved him. I think he felt people needed him, but, because of his unhappy childhood, I don't think before he had his stroke he ever felt anybody really loved him.

I said to many friends, 'When you've talked to him, take his hand and tell him that you love him.' It's strange how hard that is for some people to do. I'll never forget the day my father-in-law came into the Intensive Care Unit. He stood very close to the wall and was obviously very apprehensive. Jamie took him by the hand and said, 'Come on, Grandpa, come and hold Daddy's hand and tell him you love him.' He couldn't do it. I know Ian loves Robin and Robin loves Ian, but neither of them can drop their defences and communicate with one another.

We decided never to leave Robin alone. I thought it would be terrifying for him to regain consciousness and not see anyone he knew. Apart from two occasions when there was a really big trust meeting, I or one of the children was always with him. And on those two occasions Roger was there. Robin and Roger do not just have a master/servant relationship.

They are friends. After all, without Roger, Robin wouldn't even have got as far as the hospital.

I sat with my husband all morning after the operation and then at noon went back to St Clement Danes church for the service I'd noted the day before. I went down to the crypt and sat in the same chair as I had done the previous day. I waited for everyone else to arrive, but no one else did. I thought: There can't be a service with just me. But the clergyman arrived and started the service. I thought: How terrible. What am I going to do? I can't take Communion because I've not been confirmed.

I decided I would tell him when he got to the part of the service when he prepared the sacrament, but when the time came, I found I just couldn't. He had to take Communion himself anyway.

He came forward towards me and I found myself taking Communion for the first time. I explained quietly to God that I was very sorry, but I didn't think I could just sit there when it had been prepared.

However, I felt I couldn't leave without giving a truthful explanation to the vicar. I went upstairs and found him standing by the main door. I asked if I could speak to him. He said, 'I was waiting for you. Come into my office.'

I explained that I had got married in the church and that my husband was terribly ill and that I'd sat there all day yesterday. He said he'd seen me.

I then added that I had never been confirmed and that I knew I should not have taken Communion. He told me it was perfectly all right and offered to go and see Robin. I left the church feeling at peace.

When I arrived at the hospital on Sunday from Marbella, Carol Price gave me a copy of a prayer book called *The Daily Word*. I hadn't realised until then that she was very religious. She told me that she felt the prayers in it might help me and said she would arrange for me to have the March edition. It came on that Thursday. The February edition had a picture of a bowl of red roses on the cover, but on the cover of the March edition was a field in Kentucky full of mares and foals fenced in by white railings. I was overwhelmed. When I flew into Lexington, Kentucky for the first time, and saw mares and foals in white-fenced fields that come right up to the edge of the airfield called appropriately Blue Grass Field, I thought I must have died and gone to heaven, because to me that is what heaven will look like. And here was that very scene on the cover of a prayer book. I felt totally convinced that it was a sign from God because only He and I knew that that was my picture of heaven. Until then I'd felt that I couldn't communicate with God, maybe because He didn't want me to. But when I saw the cover of that prayer book it was as though He was telling me, 'Yes, the door is open.'

After the service Henrietta went back to the National Hospital. There were more visitors than ever.

'Normally,' said Iris Dillon, sister in charge of the Intensive Care Unit, 'we only have next of kin in the ward, which is basically immediate family and a maximum of five or six people. In Robin's case, however, there were easily thirty visitors nearly all the time and someone new popping in about every fifteen minutes. It was a major problem. We only have a small waiting-room and there were other patients with relatives to consider. Although I'll admit some of the other patients' relatives were interested to see people they had read about in the newspapers.'

Nick Hirsch felt the numbers of visitors were beginning to hamper the work of the Intensive Care Unit. 'It's a fairly small ward and the nurses are very busy and they were being constantly interrupted by visitors. Although we have a very open-door policy, the morning tends to be for getting the patient washed, physiotherapy and that sort of thing and the afternoon for visitors. In this case the sheer numbers arriving at all hours, were impeding the flow of nursing care. Some of the visitors were very hoity-toity, but as none of them knew anything about medical matters, they didn't faze me.'

Sister Queally found the sheer numbers a bit of a shock. 'In some ways they were quite different from normal people,' she said. 'Normal people, unless they are extremely anxious, wait for you to come up and tell them things, but in Robin's case, people came straight up to you or intercepted the doctors before you could give them the information they were looking for. When someone is as critically ill as Lord Tavistock was, it is of course a very traumatic time for everyone and in that respect the visitors were asking the same things as any relative would: "What's happening?", "Why are you doing that?", "Who is that doctor?" '

Henrietta became quickly aware of the problems the sheer numbers of visitors were causing.

I think at first the team in the Intensive Care Unit must have felt we were all very spoilt. But after a few days, I think the nurses came to accept us more because they realised that we weren't trying to be difficult or obstructive, but wanted to be helpful and do what was best for Robin.

As welcome as the visitors were, the strain of having quite so many was also felt by the family. 'It sounds very selfish,' said Andrew, 'but talking to them, calming them down and explaining the same thing over and over again took up a tremendous amount of time, energy and strength which we needed when we went in to see Daddy.'

A couple of practical suggestions made all the difference. Iris Dillon decided to let the Tavistocks take over the small relatives' room at the end of the ward. The majority of visitors would be kept there and a maximum of two people would visit Robin at any time. Jeni Sieff and Susan Wolfson suggested they organise a rota of friends. Some would be allocated to man the phones, others to talk to the family or other visitors and some to sit with Robin.

Henrietta
I was very conscious that it was terribly important to make people feel involved and welcome. I felt that if they were there at the beginning of Robin's illness, they would also be around later when he would really need them. Whereas if they were turned away at the beginning, they wouldn't want to get involved later on. Looking back, it was absolutely the right thing to do, but I didn't know what made me feel it so strongly then.

Susan understood that I didn't want any negative feelings around Robin, and before she compiled the rota asked me first who was not under any circumstances to sit with him.

You learn a lot about human nature by the way people behave in hospital. You're very grateful to friends for coming but they can put a tremendous amount of pressure on you and you haven't got time or energy to worry about their feelings. I've learnt a lot about how to be with someone when they have to go through something as traumatic as Robin's stroke.

The little visitors' room we sat in was only six feet by six with desperately uncomfortable wooden chairs. Sometimes there were more than a dozen of us in this tiny space and Andrew – ever since he spent so long in traction in a small room in hospital – is paranoid about tiny spaces being immaculate and before we knew he was coming everybody used to have a tremendous tidy-up. But it didn't matter how tidy we made the room, he always said, 'I don't understand how you can all sit in this pigsty,' and managed to find something to tidy up.

The number of visitors paled, however, compared to the number of telephone calls. The main hospital switchboard was constantly jammed with inquiries from friends, relatives and the media. The telephone in the Intensive Care Ward rang all the time and the staff had to repeat the condition of the patient over a hundred times a day. 'It was like having a patient with hundreds and hundreds of relatives,' said Sister Queally. 'Also because the newspapers were ringing all the time, we had to be extra careful over what we said. After a day or so we used to say, "I'll hand you over to one of the relatives," and stopped giving out any information over the telephone at all.'

There were also embarrassing moments. 'I remember one time when I felt particularly harassed,' said Sister Dillon. 'I grabbed the telephone receiver and shouted into it in a very gruff manner, "Sister speaking." The voice at the other end said, "I'm terribly sorry to bother you, but it's the Archbishop of Canterbury here." I felt terrible because the tone of my voice wasn't as it should be.' Other callers included the Aga Khan and the Duchess of Gloucester. A solution was found to this problem by organising a private telephone line, which was installed within a week.

The telephones were also ringing non-stop at Woburn Abbey and

Clarendon Place. Woburn was being manned by Lady Tavistock's PA, Meg. 'Hundreds of people were calling,' she said. 'At first we kept lists of everybody's name, but gave up after a while because there were just too many. We had calls from people who didn't know Lord Tavistock, people who had met him once or whom he had been very kind to. There were stalwarts who rang regularly and wanted a continuous story. There were some you knew you could say anything to and some you knew you couldn't. The numbers were endless.'

The telephone at Clarendon Place was manned by Roger. 'The ringing was non-stop,' he said. 'As soon as I put the receiver down, the phone would ring again. Friends, royalty, politicians, show business people like Terence Stamp and David Jacobs all wanted to know how His Lordship was. At the time I didn't realise how exhausting it all was. The housekeeper was very good and made me endless cups of coffee and I lived off bacon muffins which she bought from Marks & Spencer for me. What I told people depended on who they were. I told some people the truth and others what I thought they should know.'

It didn't take long for Jeni Sieff and Susan Wolfson to work out a rota which involved about twenty people. There was always one of the family, Henrietta, Andrew, Jamie, or Robbie, sitting with Lord Tavistock together with one other person. Robin's half-brother Francis came every day and some days more than once. 'He was terribly upset about Robin,' said Henrietta.

Henrietta sat with her husband from about 3.00 a.m. until 4.00 p.m.

I found it much easier to drive through London when there were no people about. The first time I came out of the hospital on the Monday before Robin's operation, everybody was rushing about and jumping on and off buses, whereas everything in my life had been switched off. I couldn't cope with everyone doing their same things when my life was in such a trauma. Andrew and Jamie shared the days, Robbie was allocated the nights because he is the one who goes to night-clubs. They all talked to Robin, played him music and most of all told him how much they loved him.

'I think the importance of talking to an unconscious patient cannot be over-emphasised,' said Alan Crockard. 'Sound is also one of the things that you remember about waking up or recovering from an anaesthetic. We always talk to every unconscious patient as if he was awake.'

It was a dictum that the family took to heart, although some found maintaining a one-way conversation easier than others. Henrietta found it hard to begin with.

I felt it was desperately important not to feel inhibited about talking to Robin. But because a person in Intensive Care is never on his own, it can be quite hard to say to somebody that you love them and they shouldn't worry, in front of nurses that you don't know. But again my instinct, spirit guide, God or whatever you want to call it, came to my aid and I realised that that is a very selfish attitude and one you have to get over because it is desperately important to keep talking.

Robbie had similar feelings. 'I felt stupid and embarrassed sitting with my father when there was no response, particularly when there were other people like nurses in the room. I just didn't know what to say. If someone had given me a newspaper, I could have read it to him, but actually to sit there and make conversation was very difficult.'

Roger too felt very embarrassed. 'At first I couldn't think what to say to Lord Tavistock. Then I started to talk to him about Woburn, the people who had telephoned and had called in to see how he was. Most of the time I sat talking to him he did nothing, not even flick his eyes in recognition.'

Andrew, however, found it quite easy. 'I kept saying, "I love you, Daddy. Everything will be all right." I found it much harder to say "I love you" once he opened his eyes and regained consciousness.'

Jamie, a notorious chatterbox, also found it no problem. 'I have always talked too much and here I had a passive audience. I could whisper away to my heart's content. I have always been quite inquisitive and I like fiddling with things to see how they work. The nurses taught me how to take Daddy's blood pressure and how the machines worked. The only thing I found unpleasant was when they put a tube down to suck the mucus out of his lungs.'

Robin's stepmother Lydia coped well. 'When I first saw Robin, I asked Henrietta if I could touch him and later wept my way out of the hospital to my car. I had no problems talking to him, however, usually about the past including our time in South Africa and the barbecues we had there. Although there was never even a flicker of an eye in my direction, he sometimes had the most terrible, terrifying expression on his face, which worried me.'

The person who admits to the greatest difficulty in talking to Robin was his father, the Duke of Bedford. 'I am not at all familiar with strokes and really did not know what to expect or how to cope. I sat around helplessly for hours, wanting to do something constructive to help his recovery, but I did not feel capable of reaching him. He was just not there. I tried talking to this void, but I was not good at it. There was absolutely no reaction on the surface. I love my son deeply but I could not do anything.

'I thought by the age of seventy, I was over crying over my children, but when I saw my son surrounded by so much equipment, pipes and tubes and in a coma, the love I felt for him as a little boy came flooding back. But it was a stupid moment to try to express it, so I bottled it all up as I had learnt to do as a child. My wife and I stayed a couple of weeks in London going to the hospital each day but there did not seem to be anything one could do to help a person in a coma that was not being done by the professionals, my daughter-in-law, my grandchildren and the many really wonderful friends, some who even came from America.'

Andrew tried to understand. 'I think Grandpa was very frightened. Nicole gave him the strength to come and see Daddy by not letting him know quite how bad he was. I think if he'd really known he wouldn't have come, which would have been much worse. Grandpa and Daddy have never had a close relationship and I think it made him feel guilty as a father and guilty for leaving Woburn. It is easy to be hard on him because he didn't react to Daddy's illness the way Mummy and I did, but one has got to accept that everyone is different. I also think because Daddy was so near death, it made him feel his own age.'

The Duchess of Bedford explained further. 'My husband has a terrible fear of hospitals and illness and felt inadequate, unwanted and unnecessary. The poor father of Robin was very lost and quite desperate. I did the best I could to comfort his misery and to try to find the words of hope and reassurance that he needed to hear. It was a bizarre time. Although Robin was rigid and full of tubes, he somehow looked so young and healthy. I knew he would be all right eventually and when he moved a finger I felt overjoyed and being an optimist knew he would soon recover.'

One of the regular visitors was Carol Price. When she saw the numbers of people at the hospital she decided to organise a regular supply of food. Every day the ambassador's chauffeur brought to the hospital a hamper which contained sandwiches, wine and plastic mugs engraved with the insignia of the President of the United States. Roger was sent out to buy a small fridge.

Henrietta
After a few days, the American Embassy would ring up every morning and ask, 'What would you like today?' And one just ordered one's picnic. It meant that we could offer food to anyone who came which made them feel welcome. Normally people feel very awkward in a hospital, but the food helped break down barriers, and made them feel welcome. It was invaluable.

It's one of the things I love best about Jews. You can't walk into a Jewish household and not be fed. It immediately makes you feel welcome. In fact I think I must be Jewish without knowing it. I remember Mr Ianotti, Alan Crockard's assistant during the operation, standing in the doorway one day looking at the group of people eating and saying, 'I don't know whether you're Italian or Jewish, but you're certainly not English.'

Robin, meanwhile, was totally unaware of the organisation that was mushrooming around him.

For a patient on a life support machine and unable to breathe or eat normally, good nursing care is vital and there is a one-to-one nurse/patient relationship for ventilated patients who are paralysed. 'We try to keep the same nurse with the same patient for as many days as that nurse is on duty,' said Sister Queally. 'Nurses in the Intensive Care Unit work a two-shift system where they work for twelve hours four days one week and twelve hours three days the next. From the time Robin was brought in until the day of his operation, he was looked after by one nurse and then for the next four days by another nurse.

'We also have a set routine for looking after patients. We observe them, take their pulse, blood pressure and temperature every fifteen minutes and check that all the tubes are working properly. An unconscious patient obviously can't coordinate eating and swallowing so he is fed through a tube that goes from the nose down the oesophagus into the stomach. There is also a tube that goes from the breathing machine through the mouth into the trachea and then into the lungs. This tube must be monitored all the time to make sure it does not get blocked.

'Because unconscious patients get chest infections rather easily, particularly when they are on ventilators, you have to do regular suctioning from the tubes to get rid of secretions from the chest. Physiotherapy two or three times a day both before and after an operation is absolutely essential to help avoid chest infections and to exercise the limbs. If a patient doesn't use his limbs, even for a few days, there is a risk that the joints will stiffen up. If they do, they might never get fully back to normal again. Whatever we are doing to the patient, we always make a point of talking to him as if he was awake and calling him by his first name, so that it sounds more familiar. When Lord Tavistock first arrived his admission slip just said "Lord Tavistock". When you are doing quarter-hourly observations on somebody, it's a real mouthful to say, "Lord Tavistock, can you squeeze my hand?" and "Lord Tavistock, can you open your eyes?" all the time. So we asked if we could call him Robin.' Although Lord Tavistock had always been a very formal man and almost no one had ever dared to call him Robin before, the family didn't mind at all. Roger, however, found it offensive. 'He has always been M'Lord or Lord Tavistock to me. I didn't think it was at all necessary to call him by his first name.'

Testing the reactions of an unconscious patient is very important. 'As well as saying, "Robin, can you squeeze my hand?" you have to make sure it is not merely an automatic reaction, so you must also say, "Can you release it?" as well. We change the patient's position every two hours. As well as preventing bed-sores, it helps with their chest because if you lie in the same position and are ventilated and sedated you don't take deep breaths or clear the throat as conscious people do automatically.

'Turning the patient also helps prevent blood clots developing in the legs. We also, as a matter of routine after neurosurgery, administer anti-epileptic drugs. Epilepsy can occur when brain tissue is damaged either by an initial bleed or surgery.

'We also do everything that normal people would do for themselves. We brush their teeth and clean their tongue. If you don't eat and drink normally you get white, fluffy stuff building up on the tongue. We don't want them to get an infection in their mouth.

'Unconscious patients often lie with their eyes half shut and because they can't open and close their eyes, you have to make sure that no gritty bits get into them. Every time a normal person blinks, that lubricates the eye and protects it from minute bits of dust that one can't even see. Because an unconscious person can't blink, you have to replace the natural lubrication with eye drops and artificial tears.'

The sedation and paralysing agents were administered to Robin for thirty-six hours.

'During such times,' said Alan Crockard, 'the family is understandably very anxious and emotionally very fraught. Obviously everyone wants their loved one to wake up immediately, so there has to be a bond of trust between the family and the person that they have elected to put in charge of their loved one. I think that bond is so important, because sometimes the family's emotional instincts are to do one thing, but they've got to trust the captain to make the decision.

'For four or five days after the operation I did daily lumbar punctures, to drain the blood away from his brain. There is cerebral spinal fluid all round the brain, which drains through set channels and is collected on the surface of the brain by little filters which return it to the blood system so that it can be repeatedly manufactured by the brain. After a haemorrhage the little filters get gummed up with blood and by draining the blood away, I was lessening his chances of developing hydrocephalus.' Robin was connected to a sophisticated breathing machine called Erica, which enables the user to breathe on his own, but if he stops breathing, immediately takes over. It also records the number of times it has come to the patient's rescue, so doctors can monitor the patient's progress.

Henrietta
I remember one terrible day when they said they were going to take the machine away from Robin. It was new and on trial and had to go to another hospital. They desperately wanted to keep it, but had to wait until the following year's budget before they could pay for it. I asked if the hospital bought it immediately, would they be able to keep Robin on it. I was told they could. I thought to myself: This is what money is really for. I got out my cheque book and wrote out a cheque for several thousand pounds. In the end the trustees bought it for the hospital and a few days later, when Robin no longer needed it, we saw someone else using Erica. It was a fantastic feeling.

'You can't assess how someone who has had a bleed and is in a coma is going to do post-operatively,' said Nick Hirsch. 'I look at their recovery as a clinical problem and try to create within the body the conditions that allow the brain to recover. After that I deal with the situation of a patient I want to get off the breathing machine and to wake up.

'In Robin's case, however, at the back of my mind I worried that maybe his bleed had been so catastrophic that he wouldn't be able to function mentally afterwards. It is the worst state of affairs when you clip an aneurism and the patient recovers, gets off the breathing machine, his heart and lungs are absolutely fine, but the damage from the bleed is so great that the patient is left in a vegetative state. I think it was a distinct possibility with regard to Robin. I don't know if anybody warned Henrietta that he could have been a vegetable.

'After thirty-six hours I decided to withdraw the sedation and we then had to wait for the drug to be slowly excreted out by the kidneys, after which time, hopefully, the patient would slowly begin to wake up. Obviously the sooner you move and the more you move after such a major operation, the more likely you are to make a better recovery.'

It took a total of seventy-two hours after the operation before Robin began to move. The strain of sleepless nights and anxiety over whether he would regain consciousness were beginning to take their toll on the family. 'We all did very long shifts early on,' said Andrew, 'and one night I'd absolutely had it. I was exhausted and just before I went back to Clarendon Place I looked in to see Daddy for the last time. I walked out and it all suddenly hit me. Maybe he would never get better. I felt finished. Jamie was there and he could see I'd had it. He came up to me, took my hand and said, "Don't worry, it's all going to be all right."

'I burst out crying. Jamie was only thirteen. He was amazing.'

Henrietta remained forcefully optimistic.

I refused to believe in the possibility that Robin might die. I know during the very early stages people were worried about me. They thought I'd go mad if anything happened to him. But they didn't understand. I behave in a similar way with horses. Sometimes I look at a foal and think: That's going to win the Derby. People laugh at me, but it doesn't mean that when the horse turns out to be absolutely useless, I'm going to go to pieces. Not at all. It's all to do with trying to build the best picture in the world and enjoying it. I couldn't bear to go through life thinking: Oh dear, that's probably going to be a terrible horse and win nothing. I have the best fantasy life possible. If it doesn't happen, it's not the end of the world and at least I've enjoyed the fantasy. But if you conjure up the worst possible outcome and the worst happens, it just compounds the badness.

It sounds extraordinary but I never felt sorry for Robin, even though he was so ill, because he never looked in pain. It was very different when Andrew was in hospital. The perspiration used to roll off him because he was in agony. It's far harder to be with someone you love who's in terrible pain, than if they're unconscious, because really if they're in the state that Robin was in, the only people who are suffering are those who love him. He wasn't.

Robin is the sort of man who never looks messy or dirty and

I felt that while he was unconscious he would want to look as if he had been well.

He always liked to have his nails terribly short, so every three or four days I asked our friend Francis Yam, who is hairdresser to the family, to come along and do his nails and wash and cut his hair. He looked wonderful the entire time. He often now asks me, 'What did I look like?' and I can always honestly say, 'Perfect.'

The only thing that mattered was to get Robin better and he had to have everything I could think of. We borrowed a television with a video recorder because I thought his favourite film *The Magnificent Seven* might be on or we could put on a film for him on the video.

There was a wonderful atmosphere in the Intensive Care Unit. Just like an air raid shelter. No one was trivial. Everyone did the best they could to help Robin get better.

Countess Esterhazy agrees. 'The love and care that went into getting Robin well was very touching. The way Henrietta behaved, and the children, the staff at Woburn, Roger, everyone put 150 per cent into it. Henrietta has a wonderful bunch of friends, who came round and supported her. There was a tremendous team effort. There was no question of anybody ever saying, "I'm tired, I can't go on." '

One night, however, even Henrietta's intense positiveness took a massive jolt.

I was sitting in our little waiting-room when suddenly a young doctor came in, sat down beside me and said, 'Isn't it wonderful? It looks as though he's coming out. Now all we've got to hope is that he's got comprehension.'

It unleashed terrible fear and panic in my mind and started a chain of horror that lasted several days. It was really frightening. If you have no comprehension you aren't anybody.

Does it mean he wouldn't be able to understand anything? Has he lost language? If you have lost language can you learn it again? The only similar state of panic to describe how I felt would be if you were in a foreign country where you didn't speak the language. You are arrested without knowing why and put in jail not knowing how you can ever make contact with anyone again. I felt incapable and powerless. I didn't feel there was anyone to talk to. I didn't want to put Andrew through what I was going through. The following morning when people arrived at the hospital, I didn't want to see them. I wasn't articulate enough to explain what my fears were, and if I had been, I felt no one would understand, so there was no point in talking. I felt I had been so stupid because until that moment such thoughts had never occurred to me. I knew that from Robin's point of view, if he couldn't be pretty well whole, he'd rather die. I was in a terrible dilemma. Maybe we were doing too much and maybe he should have died. Maybe we would all feel guilty about getting him to the right doctor at the right time. We were doing everything to save him, but inside myself there was a voice which said, 'Should you be doing all this?' I knew Robin would hate to be dependent on other people. He'd never wanted to rely on anybody.

I felt negative and couldn't cope for one whole day and then I forced myself to go on. I realised how grateful I was to my friends. They probably interpreted my behaviour as 'She's about to blow' and didn't put any pressure on me to do anything. They realised I had enough trouble coping with myself.

I got books and started reading all about brain damage. Seventeen friends gave me a copy of *The Man Who Mistook His Wife for a Hat* by Oliver Sacks. Nicole Bedford gave me a book called *Strokes* in which she wrote an inscription which read 'Bon Voyage'.

I discovered that you can lose short-term memory totally and it never comes back. You can be introduced to your wife and child one day and when you see them the next day you don't know who they are. Memory is chemical. The only way you have long-term memory is because you file it. I had never thought before that without your brain you are nothing. Like many people, I'd always thought of the heart as the most important organ, but you can have an artificial heart and be perfectly all right, but an artificial brain would do you no good at all, because it wouldn't be you. All we really are is a composite of our thoughts and memory.'

There was little consolation in the terrible no man's land in which Henrietta found herself. Instead of retreating into despair, however, she continued to do everything she could to help her husband get well. She felt confident that he was receiving the best possible conventional medical care, but she also harnessed every possible alternative medical treatment including using psychic powers to help him too. She was leaving nothing to chance.

Henrietta
One of Robin's daily visitors was Lord Northampton. Spenny is a medium and very psychic. Robin has always laughed at that sort of thing, but Spenny used to come to the hospital every day and sit and hold Robin's feet and talk to him. When Robin was only half-alive, Spenny said it was very difficult for him to come back as he was having such a wonderful time on the other side.

He said two people were holding him back, his mother and Philippa Chelsea, Charles's wife and a great friend of ours who died of a heart attack when she was forty-nine. He said it was only Robin's very strong sense of duty which made him come back. I did not find any of it difficult to believe.

Morgan Wheelock feels that Robin did not particularly want to return to the real world but was astounded that so many people cared for him here, and so decided to come back.

Henrietta
I had a crystal with me all the time Robin was ill. The children had theirs with them too. I held mine in my hand when I was with him and if I left the room I put it near him. I felt that as well as helping him recover, the crystals would show us the right thing to do. I feel sure they were an intrinsic part of Robin's recovery.

* * *

125

After seventy-two hours Robin began opening and closing his eyes.

At no point did I ever wonder if he knew who I was. I knew everyone else must have wondered if he recognised me or not, but I knew he did, maybe not as his wife as such, but as someone familiar.

As Robin was still connected to the life support machine he couldn't speak. It was therefore difficult to know how much comprehension he had. Henrietta felt that although he might not have understood everything people said to him, he understood the general meaning.

I felt he knew one cared. It was like an animal relationship. Lots of people constantly talk to their animals and never worry whether they understand every word or not. They know they understand the tone. I felt sure that everybody he knew was always familiar to him, which doesn't mean he knew exactly who they were. His body language with people he had never seen before was different from when they were people he knew. It's the same with horses. Certainly the ones I have really related to stiffen slightly or move differently in reaction to different people and I have always known if they knew someone or not and trusted them or not. But it's only since Robin's stroke that I realised that knowing horse body language helped me understand Robin's body language. I'm sure if I hadn't been of the earth and animals, and particularly if I hadn't spent those eleven days and nights with Mrs Moss when she was so ill, I couldn't have coped.

For a few days Robin drifted in and out of consciousness. One day the Archbishop of Canterbury telephoned me to say he was sending the Very Reverend John Petter, Provost of Coventry Cathedral, to see Robin because he had healed an enormous number of people. He asked that the boys and I were there. Robin was then in a small side-ward and I felt rather apprehensive. I thought if Robin woke up, and saw a priest at his bedside, he might think he was dying, but as soon as I saw the provost I felt comfortable. He asked Andrew,

Robbie, Jamie and I to link hands round Robin's bed. He prayed and touched Robin who was asleep. Then he went away.

Once Robin had regained consciousness, the next hurdle was to wean him off the breathing machine. This was accomplished under the direction of Nick Hirsch. 'I did a ward round every day and decided whether I was going to take Robin off the ventilator and for how long. He always had a tube down through his mouth into his trachea so that if there was any difficulty and he wasn't breathing properly we could immediately put him back on the breathing machine.'

Nick Hirsch's decisions were based on chest x-rays and a test called arterial blood gas analysis where blood is removed from an artery and tested for the amount of oxygen it contains. This reflects how the lungs are working. The timing of taking a patient off a breathing machine is crucial. Patients who have been on a life support machine can lose their swallowing reflex. There is an automatic valve between swallowing and breathing and if the valve remains open, liquid goes straight into the patient's lungs and kills him immediately. A life may be saved by a delicate operation only to be lost in seconds.

Chapter 10

'He Still Hates Bananas'

There is nothing worth the wear of winning but laughter and the love of friends.   Hillaire Belloc

The brain, which accepts messages from all the rest of the body and houses the control panel for all pain and sensitivity, is itself entirely lacking in feeling. Someone who had their brain probed while conscious could tell the surgeon, 'Yes, that hurts my leg.'

'When we do a brain operation,' said Alan Crockard, 'the patient will recover from it far quicker than if he had an operation on his leg or stomach. Not only can the brain itself not feel, but the skull bone has very few pain fibres and the sore skin covering the brain heals up in a matter of days. The headache people get is not from the brain itself, but from the coverings of the brain.'

It does, however, take longer for the brain to recover from the bruising and swelling caused by a stroke, a haemorrhage and an operation.

Although brain surgery techniques are very advanced, how the brain works remains one of the greatest mysteries of the human body. For many years doctors have tried to work out which parts of the brain control what parts of the body.

They have been able to map out the larger areas, but there is still a lot to discover. They do know that a thin area that goes over the head from ear to ear affects movement, an area at the back of the head receives and interprets vision and a spot just above the left ear initiates speech. The frontal lobes control movement, register senses and are the home of abstract mental qualities like mood,

129

drive and concentration. There is another area towards the front of the brain which if damaged has an extraordinary effect. The person will be able to move his hand and arm perfectly normally, but loses the ability to work out how these movements are combined when, for example, he puts on a jumper. Another odd thing about someone who has had a stroke is that he may not be able to speak, but his ability to appreciate music is unimpaired, as this is received in a different part of the brain.

One of the difficulties in diagnosing Robin's state was that nearly all his brain had been flooded by the haemorrhage and cleared only very slowly.

'Because of where the bleed was,' said Sister Dillon, 'we knew that Robin's speech and memory would probably be affected, but we didn't know by how much. Sometimes after such a haemorrhage the long-term memory may be intact and the patient might remember winning the egg and spoon race when he was ten, but he might not remember what he had for breakfast.'

Because Robin's haemorrhage was in the motor area which worked the right side of his body Alan Crockard was worried that he might be left with a spastic right arm and leg. There was also damage in the front lobes, the thinking, reasoning and personality bits of the brain.

Alan Crockard confirms that the personality can easily be affected by brain injury. 'The patient can wake up from the operation quite a different person. Personality is a very subtle thing. The brain damage to the personality can be minute and still make a major difference to the patient. His view of life may change by a tiny percentage, but that tiny percentage may make all the difference. A stockbroker may no longer know when to buy or sell shares, a wine expert may totally lose his interest in wine and a musician may lose his sensitivity and no longer be able to play the violin professionally. Equally someone who has been thrusting and forceful the day before a brain haemorrhage, may wake up as a very docile person because the area of the brain that made that person demanding and gave him his drive, is gone. Yet these people can go through all the IQ tests and still in theory be the same as before they were ill.'

It was to take some time before the family would know how

Robin had been affected. When he first regained consciousness his right side was paralysed, he was incontinent, he couldn't speak or feed himself, and he was blind in his left eye.

'When a patient cannot speak it is important to try all sorts of things to try to make contact,' said Alan Crockard. 'As well as being talked to, they should be sung to and given different things to smell. It is also important to associate things like touch and sound, smell and sound. This we presume is how babies learn. However, to say Robin went back to being a child is too simplistic. In the brain-injured person there is a lot of adult information stored in the brain which the patient has no access to. What one can't tell is exactly how much information there is trying to get through a locked door to get out. It is a question of trying through speech therapy, physiotherapy, music and smell to unlock the doors. The difficulty is that one doesn't know which key is the right one and which doors will remain permanently locked. In one way Robin went right back to the beginning, but we don't know how much was in there that we couldn't communicate with.'

Once Robin was able to breathe successfully on his own, the tubes were removed and he no longer had to be intravenously fed. His first proper taste was water which he was given in very small amounts to make sure his swallowing reflex was working properly. It was. Then the hospital suggested he might like some ice-cream. Henrietta rang Claridge's.

They already knew what had happened. I explained to them that he loved their vanilla ice-cream and could I possibly come round and get some?

They could not have been nicer about our request and the first thing Robin ate was Claridge's vanilla ice-cream. You've never seen an expression on someone's face like it. It was wonderful. He smacked his lips like a small child. He couldn't feed himself, so Jamie fed it to him. I felt it would be less inhibiting for Robin if Jamie did it, because he'd fed Jamie most recently.

Jamie was delighted. 'I didn't mind feeding him at all,' he said. 'At the time it seemed completely normal.'

Henrietta

It was really touching to see them. It was two spoons to Robin and one to Jamie. Robin has always adored food. You could always change him from being in a grumpy mood to a good mood by giving him something he liked to eat. In the old days there were times in the day when you knew never to ask him anything: before any meal, and particularly before breakfast, as he was likely to be hungry and therefore irritable. We had already discussed that once Robin came off the tubes, it would be hopeless giving him hospital food. Fortunately, Antonia came to help us. She had been our Portuguese housekeeper for fourteen years and had returned to Portugal a year before Robin had his stroke. She had always been very fond of my husband. I rang her to tell her about his stroke and to my amazement she was at the hospital the next day. She told us she had borrowed money from her sister, and would stay in London for two or three weeks.

I asked Sister if it would be all right for us to use the nurses' kitchen. She agreed so I asked Antonia if she would come to the hospital and make Robin a cheese soufflé – something he had always loved. The delicious smell of it cooking wafted into the Intensive Care Unit. There was a Jewish patient who had had botulism and who had been in the unit for months. He had been flying from Geneva to London with his family and had asked for Kosher food. His wife and children didn't like the look of the food but he had a mouthful and became very ill. His life had been saved, but he wouldn't eat. Although he could walk about, he still had a tube hanging out of his nose which was the only way he would be fed. But while Antonia's soufflé was cooking, his wife came up to me and asked if her husband could have some. It was the first time he'd expressed a desire to eat. I told her it wasn't strictly Kosher but she was so pleased he wanted to eat something, she told me she wasn't worried. And from then on he often shared food with Robin.

I think the Intensive Care Unit forgave us for our eccentric behaviour, because they were particularly delighted that this patient had started eating. Once Robin had got over the problem of swallowing and began to eat properly, Roy his chauffeur used to come every morning with fresh orange juice, twisty doughnuts and other delicious items from Marks & Spencer. No wonder Robin put on so much weight as he recovered. He wasn't coordinated enough to feed himself, but when it was something he liked, he'd pick it up in his fingers whether it was soufflé, scrambled egg – no matter what.

You had to make sure when you arrived with the food that you had the spoon ready to feed him and that his arms were by his side, because if you put the food down for a second even to pick up the spoon, his fingers would be in it.

As I had known Robin since we were children, I wasn't at all embarrassed or thrown by his childlike behaviour. Perhaps if we'd met in our late twenties, it might have been more difficult to understand. I think I would have been embarrassed for him. Not at the time when he was unaware, but at the next stage when he was aware.

Roger, however, did feel embarrassed. 'As soon as Lord Tavistock woke up he was like a little bird, his mouth was open and he wanted food. And he wouldn't wait. If there were other people around apart from Lady Tavistock and Andrew, I felt very embarrassed on his behalf. Although Lady Tavistock thinks differently, I don't think he knew anybody. Most of the time I sat talking to him, he did nothing, not even flicker his eyes in recognition. But there was one night about a week after his operation when I was sitting there holding his hand and talking to him about Woburn when he suddenly squeezed my hand quite hard. I really hoped he knew it was me.'

Now that Robin had regained consciousness, the numbers of visitors who came to see him and give support to the family continued to grow. Food continued to arrive every day via the American Embassy.

Henrietta
One day we were all crowded in the grey little waiting-room staring at the walls when Susan Wolfson walked in and said she had to get some posters to cheer the room up. She looked everywhere, but couldn't find any shops near the hospital that sold posters. She was finally successful in a travel agency,

where she was given a poster which she took without even looking at it. When she got back and unwrapped it, it turned out to be a coloured picture of a beach and a palm tree. It said 'Fly Free To Paradise'. We all roared with laughter.

When things are terrible you laugh more easily. To begin with we felt awfully guilty if we even smiled; we felt it was wrong, but the doctors and nurses in the Intensive Care Unit, because what they were doing was so worthwhile, were some of the happiest people I'd ever come across.

As far as I was concerned, things kept rushing into my head that I should do to help Robin's recovery and once I thought of them, I tried to do them all far too quickly. I remember I had the same problem when Andrew was in traction and in great pain. When Andrew asked if he could have a glass of water Robin would get up very slowly and pour it out very slowly. He used to say to me, 'You mustn't rush. He's in hospital all day long. You've got to try to fill every moment and he doesn't really want a glass of water that desperately, he just wants to make contact.' And although he was absolutely right, I couldn't be like that and it used to drive me mad. Robin would probably have looked after me much better than I did him. But he wasn't in charge then. He was mainly asleep.

Henrietta and Andrew, however, hardly seemed to sleep or rest. 'You went and slept for four hours and then it was your turn to go back,' explained Andrew. 'You wanted to be with Daddy, you had things to do, people to talk to. You didn't feel tired at all.' He was given unlimited leave from his firm, Tattersalls, who were very understanding and supportive. Jamie stayed with his father morning and afternoon and in all took four weeks off from school. The family had rarely spent so much concentrated time together and, as with most families in a crisis, there were stresses and strains as they saw each other in a new light. 'Andrew was always punctual when it was his turn to come on duty,' said Henrietta. 'Robbie, however, wasn't. I'm afraid it got to me a bit.'

Robbie in turn felt he wasn't always consulted about plans for his father. 'I felt a bit left out. They didn't look at me as responsible enough to deal with things. It was a hard situation to deal with.'

Jamie felt the crisis strengthened family relationships. 'We all had to lean on each other. It showed us everyone's strengths and weaknesses and we found out what each of us was really like. Mummy and I know each other very well, even to the extent of knowing what the other is thinking.'

The crisis inevitably altered the balance of relationships within the family.

Henrietta

During the time that Robin was so ill and for a long time afterwards he became one of my children. In fact I still do sometimes feel he's my husband and my child although I don't think he'd like me to feel it. Andrew became my child and my husband. I allowed Andrew to become my controller when Robin was switched off. I couldn't do without one and to some extent he has kept some of that control today.

For example, if Andrew had said to me when we were considering the timing of Robin's operation, 'Under no circumstances are you to change doctors,' I wouldn't have done it.

Andrew saw it rather differently. 'My relationship with Mummy changed because we used to talk a lot more. She asked my advice and we discussed what was going to happen. I don't think she was really leaning on me. She just needed someone to talk to. I think in a crisis one deals with everything together. One is very selfish as a unit in terms of devoting oneself to the one important thing and not wanting to deal with anything else. Mummy and I do better under pressure and to a certain extent we like inventing dramas and making things harder. It's stimulating and gives one goals. Robbie is slightly more removed. But one has to respect everyone's views and feelings and not criticise them from one's own standpoint, just because one can't understand them. One's own viewpoint isn't the only one or necessarily the right one.

'I learned tolerance from being in hospital so long myself but I wasn't at all tolerant when it came to getting what Daddy needed, the right doctor and hospital. Then one should be determined to get the best.'

Robbie felt that the crisis revealed new aspects of his family. 'I

135

talked to my grandfather on a much deeper level than I ever had before and found out that he is a very vulnerable man, he had a hard upbringing by his parents and he's managed to cover it up very well.

'He had a very hard time dealing with the situation of my father being ill and from the outside it looks as if he might not have been as supportive of my father as he should have been, but it's difficult for him to express his feelings and now that he is in his seventies, he can't change. I know he cares for him very much, he just doesn't show it. I didn't talk much to my mother at the beginning because she automatically took control and was busy managing the situation. I suppose it was her defence against realising what the situation was. We were all waiting for her to crack because she just kept going on and on, but she didn't. She let all her feelings out later but not then. I discovered that my younger brother is very mature for his age and very sensitive. I thought my older brother was incredible. He just got on with everything and coped so well that you would think he dealt with such situations every day. I also enjoyed talking to my father's brother. A lot of members of this family don't get along and I'm always trying to get everyone to talk and reconcile whatever differences they have. I've only had a little success so far. I think it is sad that it takes events like that to bring people together.'

Overall, there was a regular group of about forty people who came to the National Hospital.

Henrietta
Each one was frightened the first time they came. I'm sure they didn't really want to come, but felt that they should. It didn't matter what time you walked into the Intensive Care Unit, there was always someone there.

Johnny Gold, who is a great friend and who owns the night-club Tramp, used to come to the hospital at about 4.00 a.m. when the night-club closed. Lydia used to come at dawn because that is the time she seems to like to get up. She sat and talked to Robin for hours. What was marvellous was that everybody was there for the same reason and as nearly everybody knew each other, it was agreeable for them to come and must have helped them want to come back. The laughter from that tiny room was amazing – you would have thought it was a party. But the hospital staff didn't seem to misinterpret it.

I was touched by people who made contact through some-one else. Cynthia Crawford, the friend and PA of Margaret Thatcher, then Prime Minister, often came to visit Robin. Mrs Thatcher, who has a surprising knowledge about medical matters, always asked after him. She wanted to come and see Robin herself but since Robin's stroke happened in the middle of the nurses' pay dispute, I thought she might be stoned to death in the Intensive Care Unit. In the end she didn't come.

The Queen's stud manager Michael Oswald is also a great friend of ours. Apparently he was asked to find out if there was anything that could be done.

I kept thinking Robin wouldn't believe the numbers of people who came, wrote and telephoned.

Although Henrietta spent most of her time at the hospital looking after her husband, Roger took advantage of the few hours she spent at the family's London home in Clarendon Place to do a little looking after of his own. 'I used to try to give her a sandwich or a carton of Marks & Spencer porridge or their chocolate custard which she loved,' he said. 'I wasn't bothered what she ate, as long as she had something.'

Henrietta appreciated his care.

When I used to get back to Clarendon Place Roger would hand me the latest batch of letters and flowers, then he'd get me something to eat and tell me to have a bath. He'd turn down my bed, unplug my telephone and tell me to go to sleep. He really nannied me. He was the same with Andrew. Roger stayed up in London from February until May and then at Newmarket until July, and throughout that time he didn't live with his wife and two children whose home is in a village near Woburn. He became terribly close to us all and not at all an employee. In a way it was sad afterwards because he put us back into our place, rather than us putting him back into his.

'I have always got on very well with the family,' said Roger, 'but it was different during the crisis. I mothered Lady Tavistock a bit.' She also worried him. 'I'd often prepare two or three large gin and tonics when Lady Tavistock and Andrew came back from the hospital and I would listen while they sat and made all sorts of plans about the future, all of which included Lord Tavistock. I just couldn't believe it and it worried me because I never thought he'd live.

'Although Lady Tavistock and Andrew were both positive about his recovery, I never thought he'd pull through and then when he did I thought he'd be a cabbage and in a wheelchair. Then when he started to know things and people, I never believed it would happen.'

During the early days after he regained consciousness Robin was not doing much in terms of moving and responding to people. He could say 'Yes' and 'No' but they didn't necessarily mean 'Yes' or 'No'. He also said 'Absolutely' a lot as if he was agreeing with everything anyone said, even when it wasn't appropriate.

'He got very upset at not being able to speak properly,' said Sister Queally. 'In the beginning when we got him out of bed and started to mobilise him, he had some weakness in his right side. He slumped to one side which made him look as if he was very depressed. We could see in his face and eyes when anything was getting too much. He certainly couldn't cope if there were too many visitors at one time. He had to concentrate too hard on what was being said. But the family were easily approachable and very good at limiting visitors and only let them stay for a short time.'

At one point Robin's hand movements became spastic, which frightened Henrietta.

Alan Crockard told me that they were unlikely to be permanent and he was right. He, however, was very upset about Robin being blind in his left eye as he had managed to operate without cutting the optic nerve and didn't think it had been damaged that much.

The nursing staff were surprised at the speed of his recovery once he regained consciousness. 'He very quickly became a person who knew when he wanted to get up or go to bed, and when he wanted to eat and when he didn't,' said Sister Queally.

'He particularly didn't want to get up when he had to start physiotherapy. He found it tiring, which of course it is. We let him rest between sessions. I think we're all guilty once very sick patients start to get better, of trying to push them a little bit too hard and to make them improve in leaps and bounds. He was also very determined to eat when he wanted to, and did not, while he was here, develop a definite pattern of breakfast, lunch and tea. Whenever he wanted to eat, something would appear. It wasn't disruptive because the family were feeding him. He ate with his fingers at the time which is quite normal because coordination is very difficult.'

Nick Hirsch, however, felt that, for Henrietta, Robin's progress was very slow. 'She would notice little things that probably weren't clinically relevant, but were very important to her. His movements would improve almost imperceptibly but she would attach great importance to them. But that's fine. That's how it should be really.'

The next major step on Robin's road to recovery was to decide on a plan for rehabilitation. This was the responsibility of Alan Crockard.

'I advised the Tavistocks on when to move Robin from the National Hospital, when to consider speech therapy, when to get on to physiotherapy. Although none of these things is a life-and-death decision, I believe in having an overall plan for treatment and it was important the family listened. I know they had a lot of well-intentioned friends with a little medical knowledge who came in and interfered saying, "It's important to start this now" and "You must delay that". But to the family's credit, despite all the pressure, they trusted me, the person they had put in charge, and listened to what I said.

'My decisions on the overall plan for his recovery were, like my decision on the timing of the operation, based on instinct coupled with experience. Instinct is a very important part of being a surgeon. In these days of high technology you're still dealing with people and with people's relatives. You have to be able to size up the patient, their relatives, the overall situation, and come to a decision which you, the surgeon, and they, the family, are happy with. Often the family can be more of a problem than the patient and I try to develop a rapport. I enjoy talking to people, and getting them to trust me is every bit as important as using the right instrument for the operation. You have to weigh up how the patient is recovering. If he, for instance, has a concentration span of two or three minutes at the most, it is unlikely that intensive therapy of any sort will do much good. Also if the patient has a memory span of less than thirty seconds, the likelihood of major strides being achieved through therapy is slim. We have to decide when the person's brain is well enough to cope with therapy. It is better to do a little often until the concentration span increases. It is the same with visits by relatives. Rather than sitting and talking to the patient non-stop, it's better for a relative to go in, say a few words, then go away and come back again in a few minutes or a few hours.'

Although Henrietta and Andrew were determined that Robin would pull through the operation, staff at the Harris Intensive Care Unit who deal with life and death cases every day were not nearly so confident. Ask any medical person for an opinion and each one is likely to come up with something different. Everyone connected with Robin's operation and recovery saw his survival in a slightly different way.

'We are always being surprised by the people who survive and those who don't,' says Sister Dillon. 'It's not always what you expect. I don't analyse it. I just let Nature take its course. But I do believe that if the family are around and communicate with the sick person, play their favourite music and give them sounds they are familiar with, it really helps. It has been medically proven that hearing is the last sense to go.'

Sister Queally agrees. 'Sometimes the family can make a major difference because the patient will later say, "I heard my wife talking to me and her voice gave me the will to come back." But you can never tell. I've sometimes had people in the Intensive Care Unit who are continually stimulated by people they know and it's made no difference. Others haven't had any stimulation and have made a recovery. The will to live is very important. Henrietta's will for Robin to come through was very strong. She and other members of the family and friends all tried desperately to bring him back.'

Nick Hirsch feels the encouragement of the family and playing music contributed to Robin's improvement in the later stages, but not when he was really unconscious or just after the operation. 'I think those things boost family morale. I'm not saying they don't help, it's just difficult to prove that they do. As to helping him remember things before the haemorrhage happened, I think this is a case of natural healing. From a scientific point of view I don't think that by playing music you can reconnect the neurones that have been destroyed.' He feels Lord Tavistock mainly survived because the operation was performed earlier rather than later.

Alan Crockard believes Robin survived because, he says, 'The operation was successful, he received good medical care, obviously because of The Man upstairs and then after that, the family.' And his own part in it? 'I had been away an awful lot at that time, lecturing around the world on various aspects of brain surgery. I am sure it was fated that I was there.'

Henrietta's birthday on 5 March occurred fourteen days after Robin's stroke.

Because Robin is so organised, the children realised that he must have got me a birthday present before he became ill, but of course they couldn't ask him where it was. They searched everywhere until they eventually found it. They showed it to Robin, told him it was my birthday and asked him to give it to me. He nodded his head and they then sent me into the room. He was sitting on the bed with this box in his hand. I asked him if he wanted to give the box to me, but he shook his head, so he obviously hadn't understood what the children had said. I took it from him later. It was an amethyst heart, which he had apparently bought just after Christmas, although even now he doesn't remember buying it. What was so incredible is that a Purple Heart is a high award for bravery in America. The children thought it was extraordinary that he'd bought it, in view of what was about to happen.

Robin was progressing slowly day by day and could now be taken out of the hospital in a wheelchair to take some air in Queen Square.

Henrietta
I thought it would be a good idea for Robin to see his dog China again as soon as possible as I felt it would be a connection for him. Roger brought the dog up to London and Andrew took

Robin out into the square in his wheelchair to see her. There was no recognition between the two, which was very strange. Later on when Robin came home to Newmarket, he would take China for walks, although he had no idea who the dog was. However, by the November after his stroke, they really didn't like each other. China was a lovely dog, but she barked at Robin and obviously felt insecure about him. Perhaps she realised that Robin was the same person, but that there was something different about him. It was very sad, but she had to go.

Although Robin was improving slowly, I was still disturbed by the young doctor's comments that he hoped my husband had comprehension. As I was leaving Clarendon Place early one morning, a few days after my birthday I suddenly realised how I could find out. I went back inside and took a banana with me to the hospital. Robin has always hated bananas. When I arrived, he was sitting up so I peeled it and handed it to him. He took it, took a big bite and started to chew. Then he frowned, glared at me and flung it across the room. I was thrilled and relieved. It was confirmation that instinctively I was right, Robin was Robin. Later I saw Alan Crockard and said to him, 'Everything is perfectly all right. He is Robin. He doesn't like bananas.' If a patient's wife had said that to me, I think I would have had her committed. But Alan was fine about it. After that when people asked how Robin was I said, 'He's fine. He still hates bananas.'

Chapter 11

Learning to Live Again

Sometimes we have to get to the top of the mountain to see the shortest way up.   Edward de Bono

People who stay in hospital for some time become institutionalised and the Tavistocks were no exception. 'We found the hospital routine and rules comfortable and comforting,' said Henrietta. 'As long as we were in the hospital, we all felt safe.'

Robin had made remarkable progress. His life was no longer in danger. He was now too well to stay in the Intensive Care Unit although he still needed further hospital care. The family had to decide which hospital to move him to.

The boys and I had all learnt a lot from the nurses and knew that from the time we left Intensive Care, it was going to be us who made the rules about Robin's recovery. We felt it was important that wherever we went, we were able to have two rooms, one for Robin and one for us and all his friends. I wanted people who visited to feel a part of his recovery. We went to see the private part of the National Hospital, but it didn't have the same atmosphere as the Harris Intensive Care Unit and we didn't think he would be happy there. Andrew and I talked about it. I initially wanted him to go to a teaching hospital rather than a private hospital. I think most private hospitals are designed so that they can be turned into hotels overnight. The hospital also had to be convenient for Alan Crockard. When we next saw him, we discussed the problem

143

and decided that same day to take Robin to the Humana Hospital Wellington. It was 22 March, twenty-nine days after his stroke.

Robin could now take steps if held but couldn't really walk. His ability to speak was mainly confined to the words 'Yes', 'No' and 'Absolutely'. He was incontinent and blind in one eye.

Moving the patient from hospital to hospital was relatively straightforward. Shifting the paraphernalia that had accumulated around him – including a television, video recorder and fridge – filled a Range-Rover owned by the Tavistocks' friend Rosemary Partridge and two other cars. Henrietta organised the removal, dividing things into those that would follow Robin to the Wellington and those that would go back home. Andrew went in the ambulance with his father.

Henrietta

We arranged for Robin to have his own private nurse at the Wellington. Although in many ways he wasn't ill enough to need one, I thought it was important for him to have a one-to-one contact. He would not have benefited from having a different person doing things for him each day. He's always been someone who needed to build up relationships with people.

Robin arrived at the Wellington at 6.00 p.m. and was taken into his room on a stretcher.

We were introduced to the nurse who was assigned to us. Her name was Tania Lorking and she watched quietly as we all arrived. It must have looked like a circus. Robin got into bed. At the National he'd been in a room with a window which looked on to a well. His room at the Wellington was on the top floor and had a wonderful view over London. We hadn't thought about how he'd react to seeing the outside world again, but when he caught sight of the view, he tried to get out of bed to go to the window. He stumbled, but luckily someone caught him.

Over the next few days the family set about structuring his care. 'It made a lot of difference that none of us was frightened of hospitals or doctors and we know how hospitals work,' said Andrew. 'It's also important when you go into hospital to say what your problems are, what you want, and not let yourself be overawed. It's important to have the confidence to say, "I don't understand what this means. Can you explain it to me?" '

Henrietta

I must admit it is very useful to be a VIP at such times, but there is one disadvantage. The staff can be so terrified of anything going wrong, that they look after you in a different way – which may not be the best way. I felt it was important that the routine established at the National Hospital was continued, and I think the staff at the Wellington found me difficult. I didn't care what they thought of me, my only interest was to get things right for Robin. I obviously didn't want to offend anybody who was helping, but I know Robin well and every time I saw him resisting someone personally and not doing what he was being asked to do, it seemed sensible to change direction.

I quickly realised, however, that Tania was the perfect person for Robin. She was gentle, petite, very pretty and peaceful – the antithesis of me – you felt totally calm in her presence.

We were not so lucky with the night nurse. We were initially sent a male nurse which I was pleased about because I thought it might be easier for Robin to have a man looking after him some of the time. Unfortunately he wore an earring. Robin has always hated men who wear earrings and I wasn't sure how he would react. I was soon to find out. I arrived at the hospital one morning to be told by the male nurse that he had had an interesting night with Robin. They'd gone for a short walk along the corridor after which Robin refused to go back to his room.

Apparently he saw a bed in the corridor and got on to it and eventually the nurse had to push him back into his room on that. I was naturally concerned. When I arrived at the hospital a couple of mornings later, I walked into the sitting-room and asked the night nurse if Robin was awake. He said he didn't know as Robin had pushed all the chairs against the door and made a barricade to keep him out. I thought if Robin could manage to do that when he was so ill, he could hardly express his feelings more clearly. The night nurse had to go, but my decision didn't make me very popular.

One of the difficulties was that Robin was unable to voice his own wishes. His lack of words was a source of immense frustration for him. He was also physically very weak. He ignored his right side for about nine weeks. It was important to build up his speech and strength with intensive therapy and he was taken each day by ambulance from the north block to the south block of the hospital for physiotherapy sessions. When Henrietta went along to see how her husband was getting on she was immediately concerned by what she saw.

Robin was lying on a huge mattress on the floor, and the physiotherapist was crouching on all fours over him. I knew that would be intolerable to him. She also got very close to Robin when she spoke to him. He has always hated people talking to him in his own space. He wouldn't do anything she asked him to do and it could have seemed that he didn't understand what she was saying. Eventually she told him she realised he must be very tired and that he could go back to his room. He immediately scuttled across the mattress and on to the stretcher. Proof he understood exactly what she was saying. He just didn't want to perform.

Eventually we were sent a really pretty physiotherapist and Robin improved dramatically. Robin has always reacted well to good-looking girls.

Henrietta's next battle was over his speech therapy.

Henrietta
Most of the sessions lasted half an hour. Robin wasted most of the time by insisting on going to the loo every few minutes. It was obvious to me that all he wanted to do was escape. In the

few moments he sat still, the speech therapist put several words printed on cards in front of him. They were the names of trees, animals and utilitarian objects. He was asked to put them into groups. He just couldn't do it. He put 'spoon' with 'oak tree'.

It was the first awareness I had of how complicated the brain is, how severely Robin's brain had been affected by the stroke and how he couldn't do things that appeared to be very simple. For someone like me, who had never come into close contact with anyone who had had a stroke or a brain operation, it was very hard to understand how Robin couldn't differentiate between a tree and a spoon, yet seemed able to understand what I was saying to him. I'm sure in his mind he didn't think a spoon and a tree were the same thing, it was just that the words didn't mean anything.

It was in fact difficult to know the extent of Robin's comprehension. I realise now that at the time I wasn't having proper conversations with him. Although I was talking to him all the time and he seemed to be responding, he wasn't actually replying.

Roger felt that they were all confused by Robin's tendency to say 'Yes' and 'Absolutely' most of the time. 'At first we thought he understood everything,' he said. 'But gradually we realised that he didn't always. He was just being a lord, being very polite, just as he knew he should be.'

Andrew noticed his father's behaviour and comprehension seemed to change according to who was with him. 'He would switch on and off according to how he felt, which was sometimes very difficult on the professional people and friends who were putting in so much to help him get well. He seemed to respond better to people who talked directly to him, as opposed to those who obviously were frightened or awkward. He always responded well to Alan Crockard who had told us, "You must talk *to* the patient not *over* the patient." '

Because Robin felt such frustration at not being able to communicate or do the simplest tasks, he was initially very irritable with his nurse Tania. 'Usually agency nurses rather than hospital nurses are assigned for special care duties,' she said. 'But I was asked to look after him for his first three days. They were awful. He got cross with me and himself because he was not able to do things.' At first she didn't think she was tough enough to cope, and was in tears by the third day. She asked to be put back to a ward for a day and told the family she was having a day off.

She returned to look after Robin the following day with great trepidation, but to her surprise found that he was 'heaps better'. In fact his progress was to improve by leaps and bounds over the next few days. 'From being incontinent and not being able to stand unaided, he became continent and could walk with aid,' said Tania.

'It was fantastic. My job became much easier and more rewarding particularly as I now felt he liked and trusted me. One of the problems over his incontinence was his inability to communicate his needs. Although he could say "Yes" or "No" he was unable to differentiate between their meanings. At the very early stages one had to watch for signs of restlessness.

'Robin was naturally unaware of exactly what had happened to him. He had woken up in a strange environment, unable to speak or perform the small activities of every day. There was a strange young girl assisting him. I don't think it was surprising that he was difficult at times.'

Now that his father was conscious and out of danger, Robbie felt more at ease. 'I started to be able to handle the situation and become part of it. Although the stroke was a terrible thing to have happened, I didn't feel depressed, because the room was always full of wonderful people who gave us a lot of support. We were all trying to be positive. Andrew gave Daddy a lot of help with his physiotherapy. Because of what Andrew has been through himself, I think my father listened to him. Andrew is only a year and a half older than I am, but his own ordeal made him grow up tremendously, he's psychologically very strong and that helped with my father.'

The source of Robin's problems during the first weeks at the Wellington was his lack of awareness of his limitations. He became angry and frustrated when he attempted to do things but found the messages from his brain were not getting through. For example, he completely lost his temper when he found he could not unclip his watch. 'It was awful watching Daddy when he really wanted to say or do something and just couldn't,' said Jamie.

Robin also tired very easily and spent about 70 per cent of his first week asleep. His daily routine was as follows. Breakfast in bed at 8.00 a.m. Bath at 8.30 a.m. after which he would go back to bed and would fall asleep before he was shaved in bed. After a couple of hours' sleep he would have a session of speech therapy or physiotherapy. 'He was always bad-tempered after these sessions, perhaps he realised his limitations,' said Tania. He would then have lunch, which would be followed by another sleep. He would then have another session of physiotherapy, and then another sleep. He would have dinner at 8.00 p.m. and then get back into bed for the night.

Henrietta

It was quite different looking after Robin at the Wellington from what it had been in the Intensive Care Unit at the National Hospital. For example, at the Wellington there was a small sunken bath in the corner of the bathroom. I often helped bathe him but it was almost impossible for two people to get him in and out and he was too heavy for one person on their own. The bathroom would have been more suitable in an hotel. It wasn't designed for patients. At the National the bath was in the middle of the room to cater for however many people were needed to do their jobs. Nor did I like carpet on the floor of the bathroom. I would have preferred a flooring you could disinfect. Fortunately Robin improved so much that by the end of the week he no longer needed to be lifted in and out of the bath.

Tania was grateful for Lady Tavistock's help. 'She was much more down to earth than I would have expected,' she said. 'I really appreciated the fact that she did not hover over me, watching my every move and questioning my every action. She allowed me the space to get on with my job and establish a rapport with Robin. That is not to say she was ever unaware of the care her husband was receiving. If ever she felt something was not up to standard, she didn't hesitate to get it changed. It was also apparent to me right from the beginning, that Robin was a very private person and used to having control of his life.'

Robin lost his temper on many occasions when he couldn't get his own way. Roger remembers one incident when the Sister was adamant that Robin should have his lunch out of bed. 'I knew His Lordship didn't want to sit on a chair to have his lunch,' he said. 'He felt much safer in bed, but as Sister had insisted, I got him out of bed, helped him sit down and put a table in front of him. He was very tense.

'The first course was soup. I tried to behave as if we were at Woburn. I put the soup down in front of him. Then I turned away from him to pull up a stool to sit on before I fed him. He was at that time still trying to eat with his fingers as he found cutlery difficult to manage.

'I was just about to sit down, when suddenly he grabbed the soup bowl and threw the lot all over me shouting, "I'll bloody get you one day." He then pushed the chair away and got himself back into bed. It was marvellous. His anger had helped him speak and given him the energy to get back into bed. I wasn't upset by it at all. Before he was ill he was always the most thoughtful, generous and kind person. I've always liked him a lot and it never bothered me what I did for him.'

Robin had always liked his food and the family were delighted to see that as his health improved so did his appetite. It took a while, however, for his manners to catch up. One day Jamie made himself some crumpets in the toaster in the sitting-room and went back into his father's room to watch the television. 'Daddy was sitting on the sofa and as I walked past him he grabbed all my crumpets and started eating them. It was almost funny.'

Now that Robin was out of danger Henrietta used to arrive at the hospital at a more civilised hour than she had done at the National, although her days were just as long.

I would get there at about 6.45 a.m. before Robin woke up in the morning. I would leave in the early evening if either Robbie or Andrew were there, otherwise I stayed until Robin was going to sleep. There was always at least one of us with him all day every day.

The telephone continued to ring all the time and the sitting-room was always full of visitors.

Henrietta's favourite picture of her and Robin taken amongst the evergreens at Woburn, 1975.

Jamie's christening in the summer of 1975 with his brothers Andrew, 13 and Robbie, 12. Dr Robert Runcie, Bishop of St Albans, who later became Archbishop of Canterbury, performed the ceremony.

Andrew in hospital in New York in 1977 when he was fifteen and recovering from his near fatal car crash.

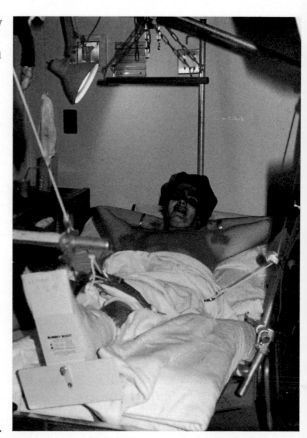

Henrietta and Robin outside Woburn, 1978.

Robin and Jamie aged six outside Woburn, 1981.

Henrietta with Mrs Moss in the park at Woburn, 1985. *Copyright Fiona Vigors*

Robin's surprise 50th birthday party two years after his stroke. On Robin's right, his father, the Duke of Bedford. Standing from left, Andrew, Jamie, his half brother Francis and Robbie, 1990.

Robin's closest friend Chuck Downer, 1990.

Robin with Roger Holmes, the butler at Woburn whose prompt action saved his life, 1990. *Copyright Graham Stark*

Robin with his three sons, from left Robbie, Jamie and Andrew. Woburn, 1990. *Copyright Graham Stark*

Robin's speech therapist Eirian Jones who taught Robin to speak and write again.

Robin and Henrietta, 1990. *Copyright Graham Stark*

'I didn't really realise how many people's lives Daddy had affected,' said Andrew, 'and how many of them saw his illness as an opportunity to give something back. We had to keep some people away because we couldn't have everyone coming at once. It was very draining on us and Daddy. We also didn't know how some people would react to him.'

Henrietta
Coming to visit Robin at the Wellington was much easier for everyone, particularly now that his life was no longer in danger. We also didn't need Carol Price's picnics any more which must have been a great relief to her staff. I don't think Robin actually knew who everyone was by name, but he certainly knew when they were familiar to him. Although he didn't remember Alan Crockard's name, he recognised his voice immediately and always responded well.

I remember one occasion when the Archbishop of Canterbury, Dr Robert Runcie, came to see Robin. He arrived earlier than expected and Robin was still half asleep. The archbishop came into the bedroom and the moment Robin saw him he jumped out of bed and stood to attention. You can't tell me that he wasn't immediately aware of who it was, although he might not have known his name. After he had gone I said to Robin by way of a test, 'Wasn't that really nice of the Pope to come and see you,' and he said quite crossly, 'Not the Pope.' So he knew.

Every day I looked for things like that, that would confirm my belief that although Robin might not be able to differentiate between a spoon and a tree, he was all there.

It was about this time that Robin wrote for the first time since his stroke. Robbie asked his father to sign his name on a menu card, which he managed to do. His memory, however, was virtually nil. He couldn't remember what had happened five minutes before unless he was given important clues. It has been one of his most long-lasting problems.

Although the family had been totally immersed in Robin's recovery, life at Woburn had to go on.

Henrietta

Visitors were still coming every day. You can't put a sign up saying 'Lord Tavistock has had a stroke. The house is closed.' Andrew went twice a week to Woburn. I didn't go for several weeks. The only thing that mattered to me was Robin's recovery. Meg, my personal assistant, was my filter. Everyone asked her questions which I now realise she would save to ask me when she thought the moment was right. The team of people there were incredible.

Andrew agreed, 'For a month anything could have happened and we wouldn't have noticed. But once it was clear that Daddy was getting better, it was a question of trying to keep things going the way Daddy would have wanted them done. I think he knew something was going to happen by the way all his papers had been left. All the details of the theme park, the Kennedy Trust and the things he was working on in London had been left very well organised and absolutely up to date. It was hard coping with normality again. I found it difficult to concentrate on small details, when we'd been so involved with an emergency. It all seemed so trivial.'

Robin's progress continued and one day Alan Crockard suggested that he should be taken home for lunch.

Henrietta

He told us to stop the car in Clarendon Place and see if he could find his own front door. There are five identical houses in the street, but Robin walked up the front steps of his own house without hesitation. Because he wasn't very steady on his feet, I was very anxious in case he fell down the stairs. Fortunately he didn't.

He wore a sports jacket for the occasion – the first time since his stroke he'd worn anything other than track-suits or pyjamas. 'When I saw him in a jacket, I realised how wrong he had looked in track-suits,' said Tania. 'He seemed to be much more himself.'

Henrietta

He couldn't, however, dress himself at all, when he first came to the Wellington. When he was given a clean pyjama top at the National, he didn't know how to put it on. Tania had to teach him what to do all over again, but it was a very long time before he could dress himself on his own. If you just gave him a pair of socks, he would merely look at them, but if you made the gesture of bending over and pulling them on to your feet, he would then be able to do it.

After a few lunches out, Alan said we could take him home for the night. I was worried about the sexual aspect of this. I realised we would be sleeping in the same bed and suddenly I felt that, in a way, Robin was a stranger. Although some of his behaviour was like a child, he was also of course still a man.

I thought maybe something would happen. Maybe it would be different. Maybe it would all go wrong. I was frightened for him and for me. I was at first too embarrassed, however, to discuss my anxieties with anyone. Finally I asked Andrew. He told me it wasn't a child's field but that he would warn Alan Crockard that I wanted to speak to him about it. Alan brought the subject up and told me not to worry and that Robin hadn't got to that stage yet. He was right. It didn't happen until months later when we were in France. We were both as nervous as when we were first together. When it was all over, Robin turned to me and said, 'It didn't make me die, did it?' I hadn't realised until he mentioned it, that he must have thought that making love might kill him. I think he believed he had suffered a heart attack, not a stroke.

We spent our first night at home with a night nurse sitting at the end of the bed. I hardly slept at all. Robin's natural time clock wasn't working at all properly. He went to the loo every hour and wanted tea and toast in the middle of the night. But it was wonderful to have him home.

A few days later, Robin was finally discharged. He had been in the Wellington for five weeks and two days. By the time he left hospital we had received over 500 letters from people. They are amazing letters, the sort you usually wouldn't read, because you would be dead. In fact Robin still hasn't read them. I think he is waiting until his memory is good enough for him not to forget a line that's written. He looks at the box we keep them in and says, 'I'm nearly ready to read them.' They are demonstrative proof that people respect and love him.

Everyone thought I would take him back to Woburn. I had initially thought I would and already had ramps built for every flight of steps in case he was in a wheelchair. I also didn't know how we could continue to live at Clarendon Place with all the stairs there too.

However, my instinct told me that he shouldn't go straight back to Woburn for several reasons. I knew Robin would never want people he had to command in the future, to see him at a total disadvantage. It would have been natural for them to retain somewhere in their mind what he was like then and they would probably always retain nagging doubts as to whether they could trust his judgement or word again. I also didn't want to remind him at that stage how much there was to do. Thirdly, I felt he might be anxious or frightened about coming back to somewhere so large. I felt we should go to our flat in Newmarket instead. We had bought the flat in 1980, after we sold our home Chevington Russell, as we felt we needed a base at Newmarket because of our involvement with horses. Andrew lives there now.

The flat is on the third floor and there isn't a lift. We were worried that Robin wouldn't be able to manage the stairs, but he had improved so much, we realised that if he took them slowly they would not be too much of a problem.

We left the Wellington to go to Newmarket on 23 April. We asked Tania if she would continue to be Robin's nurse once we left hospital and she agreed. I felt she was perfect for him. Although she was only twenty-two, had grown up on a farm in New Zealand and lived a life that was very different from Robin's, she somehow understood him perfectly. I am sure that no one else could have done it. She was an amazing young woman and I am certain she was sent to Robin to help him rebuild his life.

Even though Robin became very agitated when he could not do or say the things he wanted to, several of our friends kept telling me how much they thought he'd changed since his operation. One in particular was Bunny Esterhazy. 'He was so appreciative of everything, which he never would have been before,' she said. 'He always had good manners of course, but never showed so much warmth. Before his stroke one felt one couldn't do anything for him. He would never let you. Now it was really rather nice that at long last you could, even if it was helping him find a word he was searching for.'

Jamie, too, felt his father was 'much sweeter and happier'. Henrietta, however, didn't see her husband as being dramatically different.

Although everyone kept saying to me how much easier Robin seemed, to me he was the Robin I always knew existed, but who until his stroke he had kept firmly inside himself. What had changed was that his real self was no longer hidden. It was as if the black cloud that had always seemed to hang over him had gone. I believe that from the moment he was a conscious thinking person, his life seemed better than he had ever known it before.

Chapter 12

Home at Last

It is very good for strength to feel that someone needs you to be strong.   Elizabeth Barrett Browning

Now that Robin was out of hospital, the task of helping him remake his life began in earnest.

Henrietta
It was like arriving on an unexplored planet. Both frightening and an enormous challenge. I didn't know what he could do and what he couldn't do. I knew that the bruising in his head would take a while to clear but at that stage I couldn't foresee what would need stimulation to bring it back and what might be gone for ever. I was determined that everything possible would be done to help him make a full recovery.

When Robin came home, he was still slightly paralysed on his right side. His right hand wasn't badly affected and he could hold things, but he dragged his right foot. He was still blind in his left eye and tired easily. His main problems, however, were his speech and his memory. He still did not seem to remember what had happened five minutes earlier. He had made little progress with his speech partly because of his to-ing and fro-ing to the loo during his speech therapy sessions in hospital.

The Wellington, however, had contacted Eirian Jones, head speech therapist at Addenbrooke's Hospital, Cambridge to ask her to take Lord Tavistock as a patient, once he returned home. She works exclusively for the National Health Service and the area of Newmarket, where the Tavistocks live, comes just within the Cambridge Health District area. If they had lived a mile or two in either direction, Lord Tavistock would not have been able to become her patient. It proved to be both an inspired and lucky choice as Eirian has made a major difference to his recovery.

His first appointment was made for Monday 25 April, the first working day after his release from hospital. Until then, Robin could enjoy his first weekend home for two months. Naturally the family were nervous. He was still rather unsteady on his feet and they were anxious that he shouldn't fall. However, Henrietta and Andrew maintained their attitude of not hiding him away and his first outing was the same day that he came out of hospital.

Henrietta
We went to see Henry Cecil and his wife Julie. We had a filly called Bluebook who was running in the One Thousand Guineas that week. We were all sitting and talking when after a while Robin suddenly got up, walked out of the room and went straight to the loo. The incident eased my mind, in a similar way to the episode with the banana. To me that meant he knew where he was and there was obviously no problem with geography in his brain. I felt if he knew where the loo was in their house, he'd know where everything else was too. In fact since his stroke his sense of direction is better than it was before. I always used to navigate even if we had been somewhere several times, but now when we go to places, Robin always seems to know the way.

That evening his night nurse Maureen McNeill arrived. She was to stay until Robin stopped getting up quite so frequently during the night to go to the loo or for something to eat.

Robin had been a regular smoker before his stroke and during that weekend in Newmarket took one of Andrew's cigarettes. He broke the filter off the same way he used to and began smoking. He didn't enjoy it, however, and has not smoked since.

Robin arrived for his first appointment with Eirian accompanied by Tania. Henrietta stayed away to allow a rapport to be established between the two of them.

'I'd been told by the Wellington how severe Robin's language disorder was,' said Eirian. 'I was expecting somebody who wasn't able to communicate at all. When he arrived I said, "Good morning, Lord Tavistock. I am Eirian Jones." He replied, "Good morning. Yes, Lord Tavistock." I thought: What's this? Is he talking? I said, "Would you like a cup of tea?" He said, "I would like a cup of tea." I then said, "Would you like to wait in my office?" He said, "I would like to wait in your office." I went to make the tea and said to my colleagues, "What is going on? He *can* talk." I went into my office with the tea, did a simple test and within a few seconds realised that in fact he had a very severe case of what is called modified echolalia. This is a condition where the patient compulsively echoes what you say to him, but alters it to sound grammatically correct. There was very little Robin could say himself other than "Yes", "No" and a couple of stock phrases like "Absolutely". In fact he still occasionally uses "Absolutely". It is probably a word he liked to use before his stroke and he uses it now as a way of stalling while he's thinking of the correct word he needs.

'The echolalia itself is compulsive, but later Robin continued to use it partly as a strategy, because on the surface it made him sound more normal. He was putting on a big front. Robin comes from a social background where one is trained in the social graces and other than these graces he had very little speech at all. He had such problems finding the words he wanted to use that rather than be silent, he filled the gaps by repeating what had been said to him.

'Initially he appeared not to have any problems in understanding at all, but in fact he had massive problems. I also discovered that he could not read or write or even count up to ten.

'However, he wasn't physically handicapped, which was lucky in many ways. Many people are embarrassed and withdraw when confronted with someone who is physically handicapped. It can also, however, be a huge disadvantage. If you look normal, but suddenly start spouting nonsense or don't speak at all, the immediate assumption is that you have an intellectual deficit.'

Robin was suffering from a condition called dysphasia, a language disorder that results from damage to the language centre in the dominant hemisphere of the brain. The words have not been wiped out. They are there, but the patient can't get to them.

About 250,000 people in this country are struggling to cope with the effects of dysphasia. This includes about one-third of all stroke victims plus many others who suffer from head injuries or disease.

Dysphasia is an invisible disability but its effects can be devastating. At its most severe it can leave people completely unable to understand written or spoken language and incapable of communicating through speech, writing or gesture. It can catastrophically affect close relationships and the ability to work and communicate in social situations. Everyday activities such as using the telephone, enjoying newspapers, books, the television and radio can become impossible. Impatience and intolerance on the part of others add to the victim's misery and frustration. People suffering from dysphasia do not lose their intelligence and the frustration and anger they feel at not being able to get out a single word they want to say can be overwhelming.

The dysphasic is constantly searching for a word, which can seem to be stuck permanently on the tip of their tongue. A dysphasic trying to talk has frustrations and problems similar in kind but far worse in degree to an ordinary person trying to communicate in a foreign language he or she can hardly speak. There is not the vocabulary, subtlety of language or quickness of speech that reflects one's intelligence.

Dysphasia is in fact a relatively newly discovered condition. Before it was recognised as a physical complaint, many sufferers who were unable to express themselves or speak were misdiagnosed as being mentally confused or demented and put in mental hospitals.

Henrietta felt it was vital to give Robin every chance to learn to speak again.

If you can't communicate, you are totally a prisoner.

'Most people talk without even thinking about it,' explained Eirian, 'but a dysphasic has actually to think consciously about how and where he can find the right word. It's like going into a library, working out where the books on gardening are kept, remembering the name of the author, working out what the alphabet is and where his name comes in the alphabet. Then going along the shelves until you have found the right book, then taking it out of the bookshelf and handing it to the person at the desk. It's not surprising that a dysphasic speaks slowly. Sometimes they might only understand part of what you are saying to them, or nothing at all. And when they talk they may produce nothing, or a word closely associated to the one their brain is searching for. For example, they might say, "A saucer of tea," when they mean "a cup".

'Many patients do not, however, have a memory problem. This has been one of Robin's major difficulties. When he first came to see me his short-term, day-to-day memory was completely blank.'

Eirian's first session with Robin lasted one and a half hours. He sat still throughout without finding some excuse to leave. Eirian didn't know it then, but she had already made a major breakthrough. 'I didn't realise that he had not sat through any sessions of speech therapy in the other hospitals,' she said. 'I think he realised his limitations and found it so humiliating that he preferred to disappear.'

'I tested Robin to establish the extent of his language problems. One of the ways we understand the meaning of words is by their context, which Robin could do at a conversational level quite well. However, in one test I didn't allow him to rely on any context at all. Instead, I gave him pictures of a number of objects, then mentioned the object I wanted him to point to by saying only one word.

'One of the objects was a cup and amongst the other pictures were objects similar to a cup, like a saucer. There was also a picture of a spoon, which is not quite as similar, plus pictures of two totally unrelated objects. The idea behind the test is that if the patient doesn't manage to point to the cup, but points to the saucer or the spoon, I can see that although he hasn't quite got it right, his comprehension is much better than someone who points to something entirely irrelevant. Robin was only able to get to the distantly related object like the spoon. He couldn't even get as close as the saucer.

'He was better when a word was in a sentence, because he used the context and the tone of voice to help him. If he had been affected intellectually by his stroke, he wouldn't have been able to do this.

'I always like to see my patients as often as I can and for the first few months saw him for an hour or an hour and a half, four or five days a week. I did several more tests over the next few sessions. I could have done many more but he was failing so many that I thought it would be insensitive of me to continue to confront him with his failures. I carefully examined his ability to understand words and sentences, also his ability to name things and construct his own sentences. Many dysphasics also have the added problem of not being able to articulate their words properly, but Robin didn't have this at all.

'It became clear that not only could he not put his own thoughts down on paper, because he couldn't think of what words to write, but there were also other problems. Even when he had the word in his head, he had lost how to spell it. Nor could he write letters from dictation. Although he may have recognised the letter said to him, he couldn't remember its shape. At the same time although he was not paralysed, once he thought about it, he couldn't pick up a pen. His brain wasn't sending the necessary messages to his hand. When he wasn't thinking about it, however, he could pick up a pen quite naturally. This problem is called apraxia.

'I know he was having similar problems with ordinary everyday objects. Much of the time he would just pick up his knife and fork and eat, but other times he would look at them and not know how on earth to use them. He wouldn't know how to use his shaver either.

'In common with many other patients he also had what is known as dressing apraxia. Someone with this condition will look at a pair of trousers, know what they are and where they should go, but have not a clue how to get his body into them. He'll put them over his arm or head.

'The question I ask all the time in my therapy is not what a patient can or cannot do, although that is of course important, but why *can't* they do it? And at what point in the language process is the breakdown occurring? Then if they suddenly can do something, and dysphasics often will do something you don't expect them to be able to do, what has made the difference?

'Having done the tests with Robin, I had a hypothesis of what I thought was going on. I believed there were two problems. One was that he couldn't always understand what was being said to him. The other was that in order to say a word himself, he had to understand the full meaning of the word. When he had to rely on his own resources and there was no outside clue to meaning, he couldn't find and therefore say the word. My therapy was going to prove or disprove that hypothesis.

'For the first four or five sessions I used an approach that I have used many times with other patients. I gave him a picture with several pictures surrounding it and asked him to tell me whether each of the surrounding pictures was closely or distantly related to the middle one. It is a very useful exercise because it helps dysphasics get at the meaning of words as they make their decisions, which their brain is not doing automatically.

'I had to stop doing it with Robin, however, because he kept trying to name the objects all the time and when he couldn't the effect was often catastrophic. He got desperately upset. He would bang the table and rock himself in sheer frustration, anger and shame. It was pitiful to see.

'I knew he knew the object was a cup. He knew he knew it was a cup, but he just couldn't get at the word. He developed a stammer from the sheer effort of trying to speak. When I gave him three Scrabble tiles that spelt cup, he couldn't sort them out to make the correct shape of cup and even if by chance he arranged the tiles correctly, he didn't recognise the fact.

'He couldn't even write his name. Within a few weeks Henrietta brought some papers to show me which Robin had signed. They had presented him with a piece of paper, asked him to sign it and he had written his signature with a great flourish, exactly the same way he used to. But when I asked him to write his name out of context, he couldn't. It was something he'd done as a reflex action, completely automatically.'

Messages to do the simplest things were not getting through to Robin's brain. Tania tried to help by initiating actions for him and giving him simple instructions.

'At first he had great difficulty in picking up his knife in his right hand,' she said. 'He had to have the knife put in his hand and have the correct motion directed before the message would get through and he could carry out the task unaided. Later as he progressed, he only had to be shown what to do and then only to be told.'

Despite his obvious disabilities, Henrietta and Andrew felt it was important that Robin lived as normal a life as possible as soon as possible. On the Thursday of his first week home he went racing at

Newmarket to see Bluebook run in the One Thousand Guineas. (She managed to come last but one.)

Henrietta

Charles Chelsea, who is a member of the Jockey Club, was there and took Robin into the Jockey Club stand. A lot of people must have seen Robin that day. It has worried me since that perhaps some of them will not now let themselves accept that he could be 100 per cent again. That could be the one mistake we made in encouraging him to lead a normal life so quickly. I don't know if we perhaps overdid it and caused him harm by letting people see him who didn't understand his condition.

When something like Robin's stroke happens you can only do what you feel is right at the time. Now I think you've got to try to remove yourself from the situation and think of what it looks like from other people's points of view. Robin is very lucky, it doesn't matter if no one employs him again. But there are a lot of people who have strokes like Robin for whom it is vitally important that they continue to be employed. Maybe letting some people see them too soon will have a negative and damaging effect. It's important to look at the overall picture of the future and think about normal life however hard it might be at the time. When you are involved in something very serious, because the best comes out in people in a crisis, you somehow feel that the rest of your life is going to be on a life-and-death level and that everybody is always going to be very nice.

I don't think the British and particularly the, so called, establishment are very good at coping with something like Robin's disability. Over the next few months whenever we were at big gatherings, I watched how some people would see Robin and then vanish. Not, I think because they didn't like him, but because they were frightened and didn't know how to approach him or how he would behave.

If someone's broken their leg and you can see the plaster cast and crutches, you wouldn't avoid them, because it's an injury that is easy to understand. But the moment it's something to do with the mind, it's a very different situation. I remember my own difficulties when I was President of the Stars Organisation for Spastics in the late sixties and early seventies. I was awkward and embarrassed at first, but when you feel like that it actually means you are only thinking of yourself, which is quite wrong.

Robin's problem has been a breakdown of language not a loss of intelligence. Like many people struggling to speak a foreign language, he sometimes couldn't find the word he wanted to use at all, other times he stumbled over it or used a very simple perhaps child-like word to express himself. The difference was that his struggles were in his own language. However, many people who did come up to talk to him behaved as if they were in fact talking to a foreigner.

Henrietta
They shouted, gesticulated wildly, deliberately mispronounced words or worst of all talked down to Robin by using very childish language to him.

I've watched people say very slowly to Robin, 'You hungry?' As he has full comprehension it must be terrible for him. No wonder most stroke victims suffer from depression. Luckily Robin has not done so.

Alan Crockard warned me that it might happen, but when I told him some months after his stroke that it hadn't happened to Robin, he told me, 'There's no time limit. It could happen at any time.'

However, I realised how much more secure in himself he had become by his reaction to his father not inviting him to a party he gave for Nicole in Paris in July 1989. Ian asked our children but not Robin. To begin with we thought Robin's invitation had got lost in the post but then Andrew, who is rather like me and will attack every situation head on, rang up his grandfather and asked if Robin had been invited. Ian said he hadn't. Andrew said, 'In that case we won't be coming.' And no one in the family went. I found it quite extraordinary. When one of Robin's friends asked him why he thought he hadn't been invited Robin smiled and then pulled a face aping someone who was mentally deficient. It made me realise that he is not frightened of people thinking that about him. Some people could have been very upset.

In the beginning Robin found it very tiring to talk. It took up a tremendous amount of energy. 'I know he was exhausted after each of our sessions,' said Eirian. 'Initially his concentration was poor. I had to keep changing the tasks to keep him interested. I noticed that his level of concentration depended on how successful or unsuccessful he was with a task. If he felt a failure, his concentration was far worse and he felt physically more tired. I had to manipulate things so that he would succeed. We all attend better if we feel we are doing well. If I made his task a tiny bit more complex, his concentration could be shattered. When he did fail I told him exactly what I had been trying to help him achieve. There were times when I'm not sure that he understood the complexities of what I was explaining to him.

'In fact he probably didn't, but that wasn't so important. It was much more important that he realised that I recognised that he was intelligent and participating in his therapy as an equal. Helping dysphasics improve their use of language is not just a case of stimulation. They hear speech from their family and on the television and radio. I think constant stimulation puts too much pressure on the dysphasic to perform and can be very frustrating for them, because they are constantly being asked to do what they can't do. As regards Robin's severe memory problems, I felt that improvements in his language would give him more opportunity to tag his memory. He does store things in his memory, which some patients cannot do at all, but he cannot usually get at them again unless there is an external prompt. I don't give homework and rarely involve the marital partner. I feel it imposes a teaching relationship on a marital relationship. I remember Henrietta asked right away if there was anything she could do. I said that at this early stage it was more helpful not to practise his language at home. When Robin first started coming for therapy, I wasn't sure exactly what the problem was and when I had worked it out I wanted to treat him in a very specific and narrow way. I don't think it's a good idea for patients to constantly fail in front of their loved ones. Failing in front of a professional is humiliating enough, but a little bit easier than failing in front of your marital partner. I didn't think he needed to practise at home until much later. Dysphasia always affects not just the patient, but the family as well, because they bear the brunt of all the frustration.

'I decided I would test Robin about every four weeks. In April, he couldn't read or write at all. In fact writing did not start coming back until August when we really started working on it. There was no spontaneous recovery at all. I didn't work on his written language from the beginning because not being able to write distressed him very much and made him feel a failure. His ability to count to ten out loud came back quite soon, but other responses, which for most people return within the first few days, didn't for Robin. It was some time before I got a consistent response to phrases like "cup of . . .", "knock on the . . ." and "up and . . .".' He was very severely affected.

'At first when I showed Robin a picture of an object, he wouldn't listen to a word I said about it, he just desperately tried to tell me what it was and when he couldn't, became frustrated and upset. In the end I banned pictures and just talked to him, so he had to listen. On one occasion I told him he was going away and he was giving various people presents. I then described the presents he had chosen and he had to guess what he had decided to buy from my description.

'One was for his son, aged twenty-eight. I said, "He is always borrowing yours in the morning, because he says yours cuts cleaner than his does." By the end of that sentence he wasn't aware of what I was talking about. Then I said, "He has particularly tough stubble." I could see light was beginning to dawn. "He sometimes uses an old-fashioned cut-throat one." Suddenly he produced the word "razor". It was wonderful for him. I was doing what his brain should have done, making him knit the information together.

'On another occasion I drew a picture of a clock but he couldn't tell me what it was. I then said, "Mike's in bed, fast asleep, he's dreaming. In the dream he hears a bell and wakes up. His eyes open slowly and he sees numbers in front of him and there are two hands on a round object. This object is making a ringing, bell-like noise and he groans as he reaches out to turn it off." Immediately he came out with the word "clock". It was a back-door route but it worked. By the end of June I didn't have to give him nearly as much information and he was beginning to use his brain by himself, which he couldn't do before.

'I would have four clues to give him and ticked whichever clue he came in on. For example, I said, "Something to write with. Has a nib." He said, "Pen." Then I said, "Something to wear on your head." He immediately said, "Hat." He was, most of the time, by then getting the answer by the first or second clue. He was also beginning to speak in sentences. When he was stuck for a word I would give him the sound of the first syllable, but unlike many dysphasics this didn't often help. Although he was making good progress there were setbacks. A patient can seem to be coping well and then suddenly not be able to understand specific instructions. It often occurs when something is out of context or the object is not there in front of them. If I suddenly asked Robin to pass me something, he would often not be able to do it.

'Robin used to get very tense when Henrietta was there. Equally Henrietta epitomised what it must feel like to be the wife of a dysphasic. I remember one occasion in July 1988 when Henrietta sat in on one of our sessions.

'I gave Robin three pictures. One was of a bird above a branch, one was of a branch above a bird and the third was an unrelated picture. I asked him to show me the picture of the bird above the branch. He couldn't. He could have done it perfectly well if the opposite picture hadn't been there as well, but once it was he became totally confused. It is a common problem for dysphasics, the relationship between words becomes muddled in their mind. I gave him several others like a shoe in a box and a box in a shoe, but he failed every one. Henrietta couldn't contain herself. She said to him, "Robin, don't be so silly. Listen to what Eirian is saying to you. She is saying, 'Show me the *bird* above the *branch*.'"

'One has to sympathise and understand her feelings. There must be a strong emotional overlay of "Is this my lovely intelligent husband?" The grief is very powerful. We agreed in the end that she wasn't the best of observers because she kept talking to him and that it might be better if she didn't come. She was also very busy and had had enough heart-ache over his inadequacies without needing them to be highlighted with me.'

Henrietta

I remember the occasion vividly. I was sitting there doing my tapestry and I felt sheer terror when Robin couldn't pick out the right picture. It was the worst moment since that doctor in the National Hospital wondered about his comprehension. I couldn't understand how he found it impossible to see the difference. I also felt if he couldn't see the difference between a bird above a branch and a branch above a bird despite all his progress we seemed to have gone back to the beginning again.

Robin improved gradually. 'By August,' said Eirian, 'he was naming 60 per cent of the words. About this time I made him judge whether certain words were suitable ones to use. For example, I said, "He packed his basket for the holidays," and asked him if "basket" was the correct word. Not only did he have to understand the word "basket", but then reject it and find a similar word that was the correct one. Most people do this automatically, but it is very difficult for dysphasics.'

Robin was not only improving in his speech, his eyesight was slowly recovering too. In May Henrietta realised that his vision was beginning to return in his left eye. 'While walking with Robin one day, she covered his good eye and he did not falter in his step,' remembered Tania.

Henrietta

He couldn't see out of the centre of his eye at all, but although it was very very blurred, he could just see round the edges. I decided to take him to a faith healer.

Rosemary Partridge's husband John developed a blood clot behind his eye and lost his sight. He was going to see a faith healer called Matthew Manning and very kindly gave up one of his appointments so that Robin could go. I have never disbelieved in anything but even if I had, I knew it could do no harm. Robin was also receptive about going which he would never have been before. He's been seeing him regularly about once every three months. Matthew Manning puts his hands on Robin's head for about half an hour. Then he closes his eyes and sometimes talks to him. The most extraordinary thing is that sometimes when I am in the room with him, I have to stop myself from falling asleep.

I talked to Matthew about it and he said it often happens. He told me that once someone came to him with a problem he couldn't cure, but without knowing it, he cured a problem the partner had without even touching him. He's helped Robin a lot, as much with his mind as with his eye. Robin has said that from the time he can recall thinking again, his mind was in constant chaos and a terrible jumble. But after a session with Matthew Manning, it felt as though a very untidy room had been tidied up.

If you cover Robin's good eye now, he could certainly get about with his bad eye. He goes to the oculist every three months and they are still changing the lens in his glasses because the eye is continually improving.

Robin was never allowed to get bored. I think stimulation is very important, particularly in the early stages of recovery. A stroke patient should be read to and taken out. I believe in push, push, push with lots of rest.

Drives round the countryside became a daily routine, which Robin enjoyed very much. He'd never had time for such things before. On one of these drives he suddenly said he knew what was round the next corner. He was right. It was another sign that his long-term memory was coming back – something I had never doubted. One of the good things about someone recovering from a stroke is that you know that each improvement is for keeps.

Robin went to the cinema to see *Three Men and a Baby* which he found very funny and then to see *Crocodile Dundee*. In June we went to the theatre for the first time since his stroke to see *Easy Virtue* by Noël Coward. I chose it because it has clever, amusing dialogue, but is not too demanding. Robin loved it and laughed a lot. I realised he had total comprehension because you couldn't laugh the way he had done if you didn't understand what was being said. He didn't remember it at all the next day, however, but I don't think that mattered. He had participated in the whole thing while it was happening. At the beginning of July we went to see Maggie Smith in

Lettice and Lovage which he absolutely adored. This time he did remember bits of it and wanted to see it again.

His memory was a continual problem. Although he always knew who all of us were, he often couldn't think of our names. Before his stroke he always used to refer to me as 'Lady Tavistock' to members of staff, but since his stroke he referred to me, particularly when he couldn't remember my name, as 'my wife' or 'Henrietta'.

Having someone in the family recovering slowly from as severe a stroke as Robin had is a strain for everyone involved. Henrietta looked for ways to cope.

I find long drives very therapeutic. I can work out things in a car. I relied heavily on my friends and strangely enough, I took up riding again, which since Andrew's and Robbie's birth, I had lost my nerve to do. Henry Cecil had a lovely Arab horse called Wanda that had been his hack, but he'd retired him as he had had foot problems like Mrs Moss. He asked me if I'd have Wanda, which I happily did. I knew that Wanda had recovered and was quiet and I asked Clive Brittain, Jupiter Island's trainer, if I could keep Wanda at his stables in New-market and ride out every morning. Clive readily agreed.

As the day I was going to ride him for the first time got nearer I thought: I have been extremely stupid, I am never going to be brave enough to ride out. I arrived that first morning, about a week after Robin was home, at 5.45 a.m. I saddled and bridled the horse and then I thought: I'm an idiot. I'm too fat now, my muscles are wasted and I won't even be able to get on him. I thought I'd go round the back so that no one could see me trying to get on the horse. I took Wanda up to a gate, which I climbed and from there climbed on to the horse. I went out with the string of horses Clive was going to work that morning and rode beside him. He said that when we got to Warren Hill, about half a mile from his stables, I should canter up the sand gallop in the middle on my own and he'd meet me at the top. I was terrified. Luckily the horse wasn't very fit and was quite puffy half-way up, so it was all right.

171

Funnily enough, I wasn't at all stiff the next morning, and every morning after that I used to get to Clive's at about the same time and ride with the string until 10.30 a.m. or 11.00 a.m.

I often joined other trainers and watched their horses work. Spending some time close to the ground made me generally feel much more able to cope with any problems. I was also doing something I had always longed to do, but had neither the time nor courage to do before. And when I actually was riding I had to concentrate on what I was doing, partly because I was frightened, and I stopped worrying about Robin. I went before 6.00 a.m. because early mornings have never bothered me and Robin was only just waking up by the time I got back home. He also went to sleep very early at night and I could always have a sleep in the afternoon if I felt tired. Ordinary life had gone. I was living from day to day.

On 17 May Robin went back to Woburn for the first time since his stroke. It was a very quiet homecoming.

I didn't want a formal welcome back and asked people to make it as natural and unstressful for him as possible. Three days later we decided he was well enough to do without a night nurse. Andrew had kept the night nurse on longer than was necessary. He was very over-protective, but he probably felt that his father had been so ill that he couldn't face anything else going wrong.

Tania, however, stayed until 7 October.

As well as helping Robin, Tania helped me. I know people will say how spoilt we were having her for so long, when perhaps we didn't really need her. I'm aware that we are very lucky, but if she hadn't been there I would have had to be with Robin all the time. If I had always looked after him I think he would now feel rather uncomfortable over the times he was helpless and incontinent. I felt that for the future it was important that he had never really failed in front of me or really needed me.

Also when someone is recovering from a stroke you mustn't

get irritated or do things too quickly for them. It takes them a long time to coordinate their movements and remember how to get dressed. I would have had to do things in slow motion, which is very difficult for me.

When you have a very busy life with lots of pressures and things you have to do, because other people are dependent on you doing them, it's difficult to decide what your priorities are. I felt I had to run Woburn, but I also wanted to spend time with Robin. At the beginning friends had wanted to be part of the team, but after all these months they naturally wanted to get back to their lives. I felt Robin stood a much better chance of making a good recovery with Tania because she understood him so well. I know it was a luxury, but I feel it contributed so much to making Robin as well as he is today. He never felt rushed, he never felt incapable and he never felt alone.

Tania was also such a success because there was a certain balance in her relationship with Robin. She could show him how to rebuild his life and he could show her places and things which, because she had led a simple life in New Zealand, she had not experienced before. I remember how pleased he was to show her how to eat an artichoke. It helped make him feel in charge again.

Tania developed an extraordinary ability of knowing what Robin wanted to say when he was at a loss for words. 'Robin's ability to communicate grew rapidly,' she said, 'but not as fast as his ability to fully understand and his wish to communicate. He would get so far in a conversation and would then get stuck. For some unknown reason I was generally able to work out what it was that he wanted to say and became a kind of interpreter for him. He would sometimes get half-way in a sentence and then turn to me and let me finish it off. I probably stayed looking after him longer than I should have done. Because I was around, he didn't push himself as hard as he could because he knew that I would know what he wanted to do or say. I also think it must have affected the people he met, who probably thought he must still have been quite ill to require a full-time nurse in attendance. I think if I had not left when I did, he wouldn't have progressed as far as I know he now has.'

Henrietta

Once Robin got back to Woburn, he used to go and sit in his car. I knew he wanted to drive, and on 4 June I decided to let him drive in the park. I told Andrew who thought I was being very irresponsible, but I felt it would help him feel free and he has always loved driving. He was thrilled. The next day when I came back from somewhere I asked Roger where Robin was and he said Andrew had taken him shooting.

I was frantic, but he enjoyed that too and even managed to hit a couple of clays. It was quite funny really because Andrew thought driving a car was dangerous, but I thought giving someone a gun when you were not absolutely sure how they were going to react was crazy. It showed us how from then on things were going to be much more difficult and tiring. Robin wanted to go off and do things, but we weren't sure how much he should be allowed to do. On the one hand we wanted to protect him and on the other to encourage him to do every-thing he could to make a complete recovery.

Robin had progressed so far that I decided we would all benefit from a holiday. Robin has always enjoyed travelling and everybody kept telling me that I needed a break. It annoyed me. I knew I was tired, but there was no way I could have just gone off. We joined friends Dagmar and Jean-Louis de Gunzburg in a holiday house in St Jean Cap Ferrat, in the south of France. They had been lent the house by Sam Johnson who owns the Johnson's Wax company. We took Jamie and Tania with us. On 15 August we were sitting having breakfast on the terrace when Robin looked out across the bay and said, 'How did I get here?' We stopped dead in our tracks. What did he mean? We'd flown in and been collected at the airport. He was behaving in the same normal way as he had been the previous day. I hadn't until then thought that he hadn't understood anything or knew who we all were. I felt very confused, but obviously in his brain a cloud had suddenly lifted. Although he can hardly remember anything for nine months prior to that date, he can remember some things from the south of France onwards.

Chapter 13

Changing Roles

To reach the sun it is not enough to jump into the air.
Peter Ustinov

After two weeks at St Jean Cap Ferrat, the Tavistocks joined other friends, Arthur and Cordelia Truger, on a chartered yacht for a trip to Sardinia. Robin seemed to follow conversations with more ease and for the first time talked about the future.

'I felt he had returned to the real world,' said Tania. 'One evening he stayed up quite late talking to me about returning to the realities of everyday living. I had not known him talk about the future before. He told me he felt he needed to give Henrietta some support and let Jamie know he was back in control. He talked about ways of getting back to work without becoming so tied up that he had no time to enjoy his life.'

Despite his progress, however, he still, as he had done in hospital, occasionally pretended he was mentally handicapped. 'Robin spent two days on the boat trying to convince a friend that he was back in the real world,' remembers Tania. 'And when he couldn't, the following day he decided to pretend to be "out to lunch". He refused to shave, the only day this happened the whole time I knew him. He didn't bother to concentrate on the conversation and at lunchtime dipped crackers into vinaigrette.'

The family arrived back at Woburn on 24 August and over the next few weeks Robin made rapid improvements. 'His recovery was always progressive,' said Tania. 'It is not unusual for stroke victims to have periods of decline, but Robin never did.

There were only periods of little or no progress.'

Before Robin's stroke he and Henrietta moved regularly between their homes in Newmarket, London and Woburn and this, once again, became the pattern of their lives. Robin attended speech therapy two or three times a week at Addenbrooke's Hospital. Henrietta began to take up the reins of running Woburn, which brought stresses and strains of its own.

Henrietta

I felt guilty about the amount of time I had to work and the amount of time I was spending with Robin. Although I now love Woburn, there are so many commitments that you don't have your own life when you live there. Every morning when I woke up I thought: What should I deal with today? Were there problems with the game park, security, the golf courses, the stud, the catering department, the deer, the shops, the shooting, the farming, the forestry, the maintenance of one of the 400 cottages, or the maintenance of Woburn? Or should I spend time with Robin?

He's very lazy about taking exercise and I knew it would do him good to walk a lot. I would have loved to walk with him in the park for a couple of hours a day, but if I did, other things wouldn't have got done. Whatever I was doing I felt I should be somewhere else. I tried to live from day to day. People said to me, 'How do you cope?' It wasn't a question of how. I just had to.

I also became involved for the first time in the Bedford Estates in London. Fortunately the trustees were very helpful to me. Everything was more difficult because, although I am very strong-willed, Robin had always been the person I went to for advice and to lose that was very hard.

Henrietta couldn't even count on her husband being sympathetic and supportive.

A brain-damaged person, like a child, has no consideration whatsoever. I got very tired because I was trying hard to do Robin's job of running Woburn well so that he wouldn't feel I had let him down. Luckily because all the people who work at Woburn feel part of a team, I had a lot of help. It must be so much harder for people with very little money. If the man of the household has a stroke and can no longer be the breadwinner, the wife has to work and when she comes home, she then has to look after her husband. Nor can she expect any consideration. It must be desperately lonely if there is no one else to help or understand. At least I didn't have that. Exhaustion is the greatest enemy of anybody looking after someone who is ill.

When you're tired you don't function well. You think irrationally and lose your sense of perspective. It is ironic that people are expected to be at their most intuitive and strong just at the time when everything has gone wrong in their lives and when they are emotionally upset and physically exhausted. I realise now how important it is to pick friends and business colleagues who will help. People can be really supportive if they feel genuinely needed.

Roger felt that despite the support Lady Tavistock has had, Lord Tavistock owes a lot to her for his recovery. 'Some people say that it's been all right for her because she's had a thousand and one people running round after her and in a sense that's true. However, from the very beginning she's always been there with him, she's always been positive and has motivated everyone else who has helped in his recovery.

'Whatever else she's had to do, and there's been a lot with Woburn and all its problems, she's always thought of what Lord Tavistock would be doing when she couldn't be with him, made sure he wouldn't be on his own and that somebody would take him for a walk or a drive.'

Andrew felt a great deal of sympathy for his mother. 'It was very hard for her when Daddy was getting much better. He could be very irritable, fly off the handle and say nasty things. It was a period that lasted between six and eighteen months after his stroke. During that time Mummy needed a lot of confidence in herself and needed to draw a lot of strength from other people.

'He didn't seem to mind how she felt or notice how much she was doing or see how much she cared. He showed her no affection or love. She was only there to do things for him. Robbie, Jamie and I all felt very upset about it because she'd put everything into getting him better and it seemed she was getting nothing back. We all tried to reassure her and got quite irritated and angry with Daddy. He would say things like, "I don't care what you want to do, I want to do this." And we would say to Mummy, "Don't listen to what he's saying. He only means it in a very small isolated moment of time." He was hard on all the people who were closest to him, but as a son you can walk out and get on with your own things. It's obviously much more difficult to cope with when you're a wife and the person you're married to suddenly behaves in such a different way.

'When I tried to explain to Daddy how selfish he was being, he either ignored me, or occasionally tried to explain his point of view. He used to say, "I nearly died, so I should be able to do what I want now. I might die again tomorrow."

'We persuaded Mummy to talk to Daddy about it too, instead of keeping the hurt to herself. Eventually she began to stand her ground and explained how selfish he was being. We now realise that it was just a stage in his recovery that he had to go through, but at the time Mummy had not only to realise that he didn't mean what he said, but also to understand why he was behaving as he was and forgive him. He's changed a lot recently which is great to see.'

Henrietta adopted a very practical approach to the problem.

I could have got very upset about his lack of consideration or emotion, but I knew that wouldn't solve anything. I have always believed in dealing with what is possible to change. Instead I tried to stay positive, not think about it too much, and get on with the things I felt needed to be done. I also realised that if the whole emotional side of him had been fully developed so early in his recovery he might have become unhappy with his progress.

Alan Crockard recognises the problem as a common one. 'Anybody who recovers from a brain injury of any sort may go through, in layperson's terms, a childlike state for a while. The patient is a bit selfish, intolerant and easily irritated. These are the symptoms of a patient who is getting better and they gradually lessen. Brain-injured people get irritable partly from frustration. Toleration is an acquired social skill. A brain-injured person will, like a toddler, have instant demands and have to be trained to be more tolerant.

'All of us have been trained to respond in a reasonable way in society. If something slightly irritates us we try to modify our behaviour and if we can't, we become irritable. When we do not have a veneer of civilisation, we may behave inappropriately. After a brain injury some people can no longer tolerate noise, make snap decisions or go through reasoned arguments, none of which would have caused them any problems before. Robin got extremely cross with Henrietta and Andrew at times, but the good thing about those temper tantrums is that they don't usually last long.

'It also happens, although less often, that a brain haemorrhage releases a very tense person from his inhibitions and tensions by abolishing whatever it was inside his head that was causing him to be like that. When that is the case he will become nicer. Robin has become nicer and less irritable, but you cannot predict which way it will go.'

Despite Robin's early lack of consideration, overall Henrietta has found her husband much easier to live with.

He enjoys things so much more. It's as though he's growing up all over again and he now loves doing all the things he never used to do or let himself enjoy. One of the ways he's changed is that he now loves going to parties. When I married him, he was very anti-social and wouldn't go to parties at all. He used to work so hard and just wasn't interested.

He was also quite shy and not the type of person to say things merely for the sake of being amusing. Now we have to hide some invitations because he wants to go to every party and I'm too exhausted to go out. Sometimes when we are at a party I say, 'I'm shattered, let's go home,' and he says, 'I'm having such a wonderful time. I want to stay.' He's not inconsiderate. I think if he isn't tired, he doesn't always notice that I might be.

The first party we went to after his stroke was in September 1988. Karim Aga Khan gave a coming-out party for his daughter Zahra in Paris. It was the most beautiful ball and Robin adored it. Although he now doesn't recall it in detail, he saw with his own eyes how much he was loved. Everywhere we walked, people came up to him and hugged him. There was such joy on their faces that not only did he look like himself, but because he was no longer under pressure, he looked years younger and happier. Taking him to the party was something I did instinctively. Looking back on it, I realise I perhaps should not have taken such a risk with someone who has had such a serious stroke and if I had to go through it all again, we probably would not have gone. Equally, however, an evening like that did an enormous amount for his recovery. It was such a boost to his confidence. I'm sure some of the people there thought that I wanted to go to the party so badly that I dragged poor Robin along too. However, he enjoyed it so much that he didn't want to leave. I started suggesting we went at about 2.00 a.m. but he kept repeating, 'Not yet. Please not yet.' In the end we left at 5.00 a.m. and then only because I got quite angry and told him I was really tired.

Another big change in Robin is that he was always a really bad sleeper and had to take sleeping pills. It used to upset me because I thought it was a dangerous thing to do long-term. He used to say he needed them because once he got into bed a tickertape machine would start up in his head and run through all his problems. I, however, only used to take a sleeping pill very occasionally. Robin hasn't had a sleeping pill since his stroke and now gets into bed and falls asleep straightaway because he has no worries. He enjoys waking up each morning too. He'll get up, look out of the window and even if the weather isn't at all good, he'll say, 'How wonderful, it's raining.'

On the other hand when I get into bed a disjointed, rather nasty movie often starts in my head and I sometimes have to take pills to sleep. I wouldn't if I felt that staying awake was going to solve a problem, but it tends to be panic time rather than planning time. Everything seems so different in the middle of the night.

Robin's relationship with Roger has changed too. 'Although Lord Tavistock and I got on very well together, he never talked a lot,' he said. 'Not just to me, but to anybody. Lady Tavistock loves talking, but he was always the quiet one at the table and would listen rather than take the lead in the conversation. He was always very serious and rarely laughed. He was aware of his position, what people thought of him and how well he was succeeding at everything. He wanted people to think well of him and always wanted to do or say the right thing. He's become a much happier person since his stroke. He's often told me that he now realises how silly it was to have a life that was all work and no play.

'Nowadays I still run the house but more of my time is taken up with him. When he was in trouble, he used to come to me to sort it out. If, for example, his hands were sticky after dinner, it was difficult for him to work out that all he had to do was wash them, so he would come to me holding up his hands. I realised they were sticky and would wash them for him. When he first came back to Woburn I'd often have to remind him to clean his teeth or wash his hair. I don't think he minded. I think he realises he relies on me quite a lot for certain things. He couldn't shave himself at one time, so I used to do that for him. Then he learned to do his face, but he couldn't shave underneath his chin, so I just did that bit. He also had problems in putting on his tie. He's always worse if he's tired.

'Years before his stroke Lord Tavistock wanted peas served at every meal, because he enjoyed them so much. Then someone told him how fattening they were, and he stopped eating them. Then after his stroke he wanted peas with every meal again. He didn't remember not eating them. He never used to drink, except for an occasional glass of port at a shooting dinner, but a year or so before his stroke Lady Tavistock kept telling him that if he had a really good wine, he might find it virtually as nice as a good port and so sometimes, if it were just the two of them, he had a glass of wine with his meal. But now he doesn't drink at all and can't remember ever having drunk.

'When he came back to Woburn he was amazed at all his cupboards full of clothes. I used to say to him, "As you're not doing anything special today, you can wear slacks and a jumper." He'd say, "OK." Then I'd open the cupboard with all the jumpers in and he'd say, "Look at all these!" He would remember the ones he'd had a very long time, but not the new jumpers bought a year or so before his stroke.'

Henrietta
Robin has always loved new clothes. He's always been beautifully dressed and enjoyed shopping. Unfortunately he doesn't care about his weight any more and when I said to him, 'If you keep putting on weight none of your clothes will fit you,' he grinned and said, 'I'll get new ones that do.'

His taste in food has changed since his stroke. He used to hate spicy food, but will now eat chilli. He still hates bananas.

Robin himself was concentrating hard on his speech therapy. 'The harder dysphasics work, the more successful they become,' said Eirian Jones. 'Their performance may go off temporarily if they are tired or stressed. Robin is still very vulnerable to stresses which are not as obvious to other people as they are to him. In August 1988, I decided to start work on his writing. At that time not only could Robin not write, he couldn't even copy letters and it took a tremendous amount of work to help him overcome that. I gave him a very simple word and asked him to fill in the last letter. He couldn't. He couldn't recall letters because he had no spelling ability. I helped him by giving him three letters and asking him to choose one. That worked a little better. We did things like tracing shapes of letters with his fingers on a stencil. I'd hold his hand and say the letter, make him repeat the name of the letter, then trace the shape. I guided his hand as we traced letters with tracing paper.

'We filled in letter shapes with a crayon like a child would do to help him get the feel of the movements of the shapes. I helped him grasp the differences in the shape of letters by giving him "b", "p", "c" and "g" and getting him to judge where he thought the various letters were alike and where they were not. It made him look carefully at the letter shapes and notice their differences. I gave him a capital letter like "A" and he'd have to select out of three small letters, "a", "x" and "t", the one that matched.

'This was difficult because he had to remember that the shape of the capital was an "A", then remember its name, look at the other three small letters and decide, although it didn't have the same shape, which of them matched the capital letter. The added difficulty is that a small "a" doesn't look at all like a capital "A". In order to do it correctly, he had to match the shapes with the letter name in his brain. Then I progressed to drawing a picture of a box and writing the word "bax" underneath it and waited to see if he recognised the incorrect spelling. He knew it was wrong, but he couldn't write an "o" by himself, so I drew an "o" for him and asked him to copy it. He couldn't unless I held and guided his hand.

'At the same time I was working on his spoken language and helping him increase his word-finding ability. By September 1988 he had progressed to the point where I could ask him to sort out words not only into the same category, but in some kind of order. He was very good at it. He was, for example, able to sort out 'second', 'minute', 'hour', 'day', 'week' in the right order from the smallest to the largest.

'Robin's spontaneous speech was by this time much better, conversation became much easier for him, because talking with another person would stimulate him to be able to select the right words in his mind. When he had to initiate speech entirely by himself he still had problems.

'Verbs are one of the most difficult areas for dysphasics and Robin had tremendous problems finding the specific verb he needed. He would use a general rather than specific verb. For example, instead of the word "to write" he would say "move the pen on the paper".

'By the end of 1988 he succeeded in naming all the objects I placed in front of him 100 per cent and during the following year continued to progress enormously with his spoken language. Now his writing is very much better too, although he still finds spelling difficult. Apparently he did not spell very well before his stroke either.

'He finds it particularly difficult when I spell a word out loud to him and ask him to write it down, because he has not only to hold the sounds of the word in his head, but also to recall the shape of the letters and how you write them. When a word has several syllables, like "disconcerting" he tends to condense it down to its first and last syllables, because he can't remember what goes in between. Interestingly enough, his writing apparently looks just as it did before his stroke – proof that it isn't a case of relearning, but of getting access to the part of the brain where writing ability is stored. If he had relearnt how to write, his writing would have no doubt looked more like mine, because that is what he has learned from.

'Many patients who have had head injuries, particularly where there has been front lobe damage, lose the ability to make judgements. At one time I thought Robin had no concept of the implications of his problem, because he would sometimes be euphoric. If I asked him how he was feeling, he would say, ''Absolutely marvellous. Fantastic. Life is wonderful. No worries at all.''

'However, I noticed he stopped being so euphoric towards the end of 1989 and I began to realise he was developing an anxiety about himself and becoming more concerned about Woburn. I feel this anxiety is a sign of his progress, because he has become more aware of his limitations and made an intellectual judgement about his problems. Most dysphasics get terrible depression, and a lot of our training involves counselling. A patient's emotional well-being is very important to his recovery of language and we often develop a similar relationship with a patient to that of a psychotherapist.

'Robin, however, hasn't been terribly depressed and I don't think he will become so. Nor will he become the negative person he was before his stroke. He is so thankful to be alive. I think he now has a different perspective on himself. He has told me that he thinks he has fundamentally changed as a person.

'However, although nobody can see they are handicapped, every dysphasic goes through a period of feeling inadequate, inept and a burden. When they feel anxious their word-finding problems become worse. They might say the wrong word or nothing at all and the person talking to them might think they are inane. Robin's intellect is intact, but he still has word-finding difficulties.

'His short-term memory is a problem too. It can be helped by giving him prompts. Sometimes he remembers partially after a prompt, sometimes completely. After a trauma like Robin has had, some people feel they have been given a new role in life. I don't think he sees the future clearly yet. He has told me, however, that he doesn't ever want to go back to being on a treadmill.

'I have told him that the fact that he is rich compared to the majority of people isn't helping because it doesn't give him the necessity or the motivation to work. He has recently said that he wants to use his recovery to help other people in a similar situation to himself, which I think is an attitude that is quite new to him.'

Although Robin's physical health was improving well, Henrietta and the family noticed that his left eye was out of alignment.

Henrietta
When he looked at you, the left eye tended to wander about. Although his sight wasn't affected in any way I felt that it was cosmetically essential to do something about it. Other people were bound to be affected when they looked at him and that wouldn't help his ability to communicate. He had an operation on his eye in October 1988 to tie it back in. He recovered quickly.

'Now that Robin was so much better, we all tried to talk him into a more healthy life-style,' said Tania. 'We tried to encourage him to eat less foods containing cholesterol and increase his exercising. Both these tasks have proved to be very difficult to accomplish. His theory is that he has cheated death once without having enjoyed his full potential of fun and happiness, and now he wants to enjoy his life to the maximum which includes eating the food he likes and doing relatively little exercise.'

By October 1988 there was no longer any medical need for Tania.

Henrietta
I didn't really want her to go. She had become so much part of our family. I suggested that when she went back to work in the hospital, she might like to continue living in our house in London. She did so and didn't leave until February 1990. It was very nice for Robin because although she was no longer looking after him, when he went to London she was there and they often went out to dinner.

It was much harder for me once Tania had gone. When she was with us I knew I could always say, 'I've got to do this, that and the other. Could you do this?' Once she had gone and for a long while afterwards, I worried about Robin as a parent would. For a time I had four boys.

185

Chapter 14

A Year Ahead

The sunset is the only way to another sunrise.   G A Parkinson

Henrietta found 1989 much more difficult to cope with than 1988.

Henrietta
The first year of Robin's illness was like wartime. Triviality
didn't count. When you have very little choice, life is very
straightforward. Once we were into the second year of Robin's
recovery, life became more complicated and therefore much
harder. There was less sympathy because people thought
Robin was so much better that there was nothing to worry
about any more and naturally wanted to get back to their own
lives.

The other thing that made 1989 much sadder was that my
mother died in April. Robin, Jamie and I had gone on holiday
and taken Roger, his wife and two sons with us as a way of
saying 'thank you' to Roger's family who had been without
him for so many months while he cared for Robin. We had
spent ten marvellous days in the Caribbean and then went on
to Disney World. It has been the last occasion when I spent a
day feeling that something somewhere was very wrong. I rang
Andrew who was in America at the time and he said rather
defensively, 'Why are you calling me?' I said, 'I don't know
really, but I have a terrible feeling that something is wrong.'

It turned out that ten minutes earlier Meg had rung him to

ask him to ring me as she had had a call to say that my mother was dying. I immediately called Daddy in Spain, but by the time I got through she had died. We left Roger and his family in Disney World and immediately took a flight to London, changed planes and went straight on to Spain. Daddy is now on his own and although he says he's not a child, as his only daughter I feel very responsible for him. It's difficult seeing him as often as I'd like to because he lives abroad, and I have to find several clear days to be able to visit him.

About eighteen months after Robin's stroke Alan Crockard sent a medical certificate to the authorities to say Robin was fit to drive and we asked for his driving licence back. Curiously once people knew he was driving again, they assumed he was 100 per cent better and found it hard to believe when I told them he was still going for speech therapy. There is such ignorance about strokes, which I suppose is not surprising. If you haven't been involved with something yourself you often don't know anything about it.

Roger went with Lord Tavistock the first time he drove himself to the speech therapist and found the experience quite nerve-racking. 'Lady Tavistock had taken him around and about, but I was very nervous that first day. I felt we were approaching a couple of roundabouts a little too fast and thought for a few seconds we might go over them instead of round them. But he knew exactly what to do and apologised for going too fast. Once all the bad parts of his stroke were in the past, a lot of his recovery has actually been fun.'

Andrew was very anxious about his father's driving too. 'I found it terrifying but I realised we had to let him try to do everything he had done before. Even now when he leaves one place to go to another we still ring and make sure he's all right. Fortunately he has a telephone in the car and we can talk to him whenever we want to.'

Although Henrietta was very keen for Robin to maintain close contacts with good friends throughout his illness, her instincts told her to protect him from people who were merely acquaintances.

I didn't want them to come into contact with him too soon.

Most people who know anything about a stroke believe that all the improvements happen in the first year and after that there is no progress at all. Whenever I could I tried to convince people that it wasn't true, but I felt I had to protect him from coming into contact with people who had closed minds on the subject. If some of them had seen him when he was not being very articulate, they could have formed a picture in their minds of his limitations. And he would have remained freeze-framed at that stage in their minds. They would also tell other people about him who in turn would form the same fixed picture in their minds too. Even if they saw him months later and he was much better, they probably wouldn't have told all the same people about his improvements.

Robin became much less inhibited. If we were out for dinner and there was something he didn't like he would actually say so. Which is not something you would normally say to your hostess. Or if a particularly fat or ugly person went by he would remark out loud on that too. It was the sort of behaviour one would normally associate with someone very young or very old.

I have wondered whether, since Robin's stroke, some people have thought: Shall we invite the Tavistocks to dinner? And then thought: I'm not sure who I shall sit Robin next to. No, let's not. They are probably worried, nervous and a little bit frightened about how to deal with him and what to say.

I personally wouldn't mind if I never went to another ball or big dinner again. Luckily I lead a very varied life. I can go to a glamorous party one evening and the next morning have to be up at 6.00 a.m. to take a mare somewhere in the horse-box. I'm lucky too that my friends are very varied and my happiest evenings are spent seeing and talking to people I instinctively feel at ease with. But it would make me sad for Robin. I feel most comfortable with people who are closest to the earth. People who are involved with Nature are, as a rule, less cruel to others than anyone else. The more sophisticated people are the more cruel some of them can be.

Since Robin's stroke I have become much more aware of my psychic powers and my instinct. I can be chatting to someone

189

quite politely or be in a room full of people and I am aware of what is happening on another dimension. It's quite tiring. I can also suddenly get a feeling of anxiety about something that I haven't thought about for days. I take it as a warning and stop doing what I'm doing and become involved in what has come into my mind. Two or three times recently my feelings have proved so accurate that I don't know what would have happened if I hadn't got involved when I did.

In order to deal with the work I have to do, I get to my desk most mornings at 6.30 a.m. and sometimes work until 11.00 p.m. I stop for dinner and then go back. Because my office is next to my bedroom I often go to my desk in the middle of the night. If I can't sleep, there is no point in lying in bed, getting myself into a state. Robin used to do this too, but happily for him now sleeps peacefully through the night.

Before his stroke Robin always acted as my brakes. He knew what would trigger me off and he'd either kick me under the table or have me under control before the explosion. I recognise now that in order to cope with everything I have become rather dictatorial. When I have too much to do and there hasn't been time to explain gently why something can't be done in one particular way and must be done in another, I can scythe right through what people have done and say 'I think that looks dreadful' and walk off. It is particularly unforgivable because a lot of the people who work at Woburn are quite exceptional: they have not treated it as their job. They behave as if it is a family business and they are an integral part of the team. I'm trying to handle things better now and have put in new brake-linings of my own.

Meg thinks Lady Tavistock now does far too much work. 'There are a lot of people to do things for her, but she is very quick-witted and goes at everything at one hundred miles an hour. Before Lord Tavistock's stroke, Lady Tavistock's responsibilities were whatever he allowed her to have and she wasn't on a completely free rein. If there was something she had done that Lord Tavistock didn't like, it would immediately be undone and reversed.

'There are millions of problems in running Woburn and I know she feels that it is her responsibility when something goes wrong. However, I don't know whether another part of her says, "I can do this better than everyone else put together" which is probably true. She also doesn't want Lord Tavistock to admit that he isn't capable of doing what he could do, nor does she want to put Andrew in the position of having to run Woburn while he is still a young man and also has a very responsible job of his own.'

Henrietta admits to feeling the strain.

I have had days at Woburn when I feel low and that I'm not accomplishing anything, that I don't have time to do anything properly, am trying to do too much, getting nowhere and don't know enough about what I'm doing. I have felt that if I go anywhere on the estate and see anyone, they will all want to ask me questions and I feel I can't cope with any more. If you are a strong person and people think you can cope, there seems to be no limit to what is piled on to you. There have been times when I've been so tired that I've felt I've been losing my grip and end up feeling sorry for myself. Meg's very understanding and panders to me a bit. They are usually the days when I feel I have been deserted by my spirit guides. I usually go to bed and wait for them to come back. When they do, it doesn't mean that my day will be perfect, but everything rolls along and I feel I can change gear properly. When things go well, I can't imagine what it's like for them to go wrong. And when they go wrong, I can't imagine how they will ever go right again.

I have, at times, needed to have some escape and be on my own. I kept being told to get away and have a rest, but I find it difficult to go on holiday in case things go wrong. Instead I have bought a tiny two-bedroomed flintstone thatched cottage near Newmarket, which I'd seen and thought about for twenty-five years. We'd all referred to it as my retirement home. It has the most wonderful view and before I owned it or even saw inside, I felt that no matter what problem you had, if you sat and looked at that view, it would somehow be solved. When Andrew told me in April 1989 that the cottage was on the market I went to look at it. The minute I saw it, I knew it was a place where I could recharge my batteries and feel able to cope with everything.

I also realise how very privileged we are to live in a house like Woburn and look out on a 3000-acre park surrounded by all the beautiful things that are there.

A lot of things have been done at Woburn since Robin's stroke and every now and again I look at something and think: My goodness. How have I managed to do all that? How have I found time to fit all this in? I heard Robin say to someone the other day, 'More has happened since I've been ill, than used to happen when I did it all.' I suppose it is because every one of us has been so keen not to slip back, that we have possibly accomplished more in less time. I have tried to keep ahead of myself. That way if something wonderful crops up that I'd like to do, I can.

I like the fact that I have been quite efficient at taking over, I've become really interested and there are lots of things I'd like to do. But I know it's not my job, it's my husband's or Andrew's.

Woburn will never belong to a woman and will never pass through the female line. Therefore all the time, I keep thinking: I mustn't get too involved in this. And: I mustn't let people think they must always come to me. That's why when any of the people who work at Woburn ask me something, I usually say, 'I will talk to Lord Tavistock about it.' I do talk to Robin about everything, although not necessarily on the day it has happened. He is interested but not worried. When I tell him things that worry me, and that would have worried him before his stroke, he tells me exactly what to do, but he's not anxious. I feel I can lean on him, but I'm not sure whether I censor my leaning. I don't think I've yet asked him something I didn't feel confident he could cope with.

My main concern for him is that he doesn't ever feel inadequate. The moment he does, I think he might stop improving. I've often heard him say to someone, 'I'm not doing that yet, but give me until Christmas and I will.' I don't think he feels that there is anything he won't ever be able to do again. I don't know if there is or not, because I'm not going to ask anybody or even myself. I don't believe in asking questions there can be no answer to. They won't change anything.

Of course I would ask Alan Crockard or Eirian Jones medically based questions like 'Is it dangerous for him to do this or that?' But never the question 'How far, at best, do you think he will go?' They could only give me an answer based on previous experience, which would be an average. I know that as far as the brain goes there is still much that is unknown.

The most important thing for someone who's had a stroke is to develop strong lines of communication. Robin and I communicate with each other far more since his stroke than we did before. Because we both had confidence in each other, knew what we were aiming for in life and knew we loved the children, we took a lot for granted. The only time we really used to talk was in the car. Now, I suppose because it is more difficult, we both take more trouble and talk much more. Sometimes when people look at me, I can tell they are thinking: Poor thing, you've been through such a hard time. But I don't see it like that. It may sound strange, but in many ways it's been a wonderful time. Of course I feel his frustration when he's trying to say something to someone and they cannot understand. I do realise how irritating it must be and feel sorry for him, but I don't pity him. I know that he is so much happier now than he has ever been.

In a way Robin's stroke has brought out the best in me. I suppose because it's made me realise how much I love him. If I didn't love him it would have probably made me feel resentful. Instead I feel we have been allowed to start again. We are cutting out a lot of trivia in our lives. It's as though we've managed to stop the car before it went over the cliff.

Chapter 15

Looking Towards the Future

We are going on swinging bravely forward along the grand high road and already behind the distant mountains is the promise of the sun.

Winston Churchill

Robin's recovery has been little less than miraculous. His progress from being six hours away from death to his current state of health has surpassed most expectations. There are still, however, several question marks over his future.

Alan Crockard believes that, 'After a stroke about 80 per cent of the recovery that will be made occurs in the first six months. The remaining 20 per cent follows over the next two to five years. I think it's fair to say that around that time, that is pretty nearly it. Robin's recovery has been incredible. His main problem is his short-term memory. Although he does now remember events that happened just a few days ago and people's names, neither of which he could do earlier in his recovery, it is open to question whether it will ever recover 100 per cent. There are various ways of getting round this, however, like keeping a diary and every evening writing down a synopsis of the day.

'As far as the future goes the chances of him having another aneurism are remote provided there are no major problems with, for example, blood pressure. We will, in any event, do another brain scan in a year or two. This is standard procedure with all patients who have had a brain haemorrhage if there is a suggestion that there might be a weakness on a blood vessel elsewhere.'

While Eirian Jones agrees about Robin's memory problems, she takes a very positive line over his intellectual abilities. 'Robin's intellect is intact and he can make decisions,' she says. 'He will, however, always have permanent memory problems, and will have to learn to accommodate them. By October 1990 his word-finding difficulty was still there, but minuscule compared to what it was.

'It has improved so much that many people have told me that they couldn't hear anything wrong with him.

'His writing and spelling have improved markedly. He can now write his own speeches as he did when as patron of the Cambridge branch of the Action for Dysphasic Adults he was called upon to inaugurate this new branch of the charity. Knowing how severely affected he was initially, I have been thrilled for him. His success owes much to his determination and the support of his family.

'The one problem he has with decision-making is that in order to make a decision, one has to consider all the aspects involved. When Robin's memory lets him down and he forgets one of the aspects, it can lead him to make the wrong decision. I see no reason why someone else couldn't give him all the points involved and make sure he remembers them, so he can then make his own decision. I believe he needs to be challenged more than he has been. Intellectually he could be involved in the running of Woburn again. First, however, in order to discover his limitations, he needs to handle a job relating to Woburn on his own, where it wouldn't be catastrophic if he made the wrong decision.

'Taking back the reins of their work is a problem for many stroke patients, particularly if their wives have successfully stood in for them while they have been ill. When someone takes over another person's work there's always a mixture of resentment, because it can be a lot of responsibility and is very tiring, and pleasure, because it is always nice to do something well.'

One of the early ways the family gently encouraged Robin to develop a sense of responsibility was to get him a dog.

Henrietta
In August 1989 Nicky Phillips, who is one of our trustees and comes shooting with us, told us that his spaniel had just had some puppies and suggested it would be a very good idea for Robin to have one. He thought it would be something for him to look after and be responsible for. Robin has always loved Nicky's spaniel Swift. She is black, very small and has an

incredible zest for life. Andrew, Robbie, Jamie, Robin and I all went to Luton Hoo where Nicky lives, to look at the puppies. Robin picked a tiny one that was really shy and kept hiding. We collected her when she was eight weeks old and have called her Slipper.

Before his stroke he was very strict with his dogs. They weren't allowed to get on chairs and certainly didn't sleep on the bed. This time, however, for the first six weeks she was with us, she slept on the pillow and now always sits by him at lunch. Slipper's been a great success and he adores her.

I realise I give Robin the consideration I would give a child, which you don't normally give your husband. I might not always answer a question the same way I used to because there might be something fearful in too direct an answer. If we are at a dinner party and I hear someone ask him a question and I hear him give an answer that is possibly not quite what he means, I can't bear the thought that they might undervalue him because of it. I manage to stop myself going up to them straightaway and explaining. But I always go up afterwards and say, 'I don't know if you know but my husband had a very serious stroke and talking English to him is a bit like talking a foreign language and he can't always find the right idiom.'

Sometimes Robin says to me, 'Why do you tell everybody?' I know I still over-protect him. I never thought I would have to protect him from anyone apart from his father. From my point of view I don't mind if people say, 'Poor Henrietta, she's married to an idiot now,' because I know I'm not. But I worry for Robin when they underestimate his level of comprehension. Many people still either talk to him very slowly as if to a child or else shout because they think he will understand better. Sometimes if he is asked a question that he knows is going to require a huge effort to reply to, he still gets lazy and says, 'Absolutely.'

Recently he has begun to stop me being too over-protective and one day he'll give me a look and I won't do it any more. In a way I think he's quite liked being protected. He never was when he was young. He has also enjoyed being self-indulgent because he's never been able to be before either. I think we both know that at a certain point it's got to stop, but what he really loves at the moment is friends to come round and bring him chocolates. If you say to him, 'You risk having a heart attack,' he says, 'I don't mind if I go tomorrow.' It's difficult to make him lose weight and take exercise. If I tell him someone has died, he will ask how and if they died in their sleep he always says, 'How wonderful.' He's not at all frightened of dying. I know he's seen something that I haven't. He doesn't seem to plan for the future.

Alan Crockard feels Robin's fundamentally different attitude to life has been brought about partly by his stroke and partly by his own decision. 'Although personality can be affected by a brain injury,' he says, 'Robin may also have changed because when you've been doing as much work as he was and you've come almost to death, I would have thought you would look at life slightly differently. He's jolly glad to wake up each day and perhaps appreciates the things around him more than he used to.'

In January 1990, Henrietta decided to mark Robin's fiftieth birthday with a big party.

Because Robin had never had a party when he was a child we decided to make it like a children's party. It was a complete surprise and Robin had no idea what we were planning. We had a dinner party at Woburn the previous evening and some guests stayed over. Robin opened his presents on the morning of his birthday and we asked about ten people to arrive at lunchtime at the house. One of the guests asked if he would show him where we had kept the Canova and Robin took him to the Sculpture Gallery where unknown to him about 200 guests were waiting. We had been told that he was on his way and everyone stayed absolutely silent until he walked in when we all sang 'Happy Birthday'. I have never seen anybody's face like it. He saw his father over the tops of people's heads and was obviously thrilled that he was there too. I have never seen Ian sweeter to Robin. A lot of the people there hadn't seen him since his stroke and you could see the relief on their faces when he obviously knew who they all were.

There was a giant cut-out steam train six feet by four, suspended from the middle of the room, that had painted on both sides 'Happy Birthday Robin', and lots of balloons. We had clowns, conjurors, jugglers, stilt-walkers and a hurdy-gurdy with a dog. Instead of having flowers in the middle of every table we had heaps of little packets of lots of delicious things to eat like Twiglets, Smarties and fairy biscuits. We served children's food like chicken drumsticks, baked beans, fish fingers and sausages. We had invited a tremendous mixture of people and they all tucked in to everything with great enthusiasm. The food had the wonderful effect of removing any formality.

I'm sure that in view of what had happened to Robin some people might have thought that the party was in bad taste and that I was treating him as a child in front of everyone. But I don't think of Robin as a child. I had also grown up knowing he had always wanted a proper child's birthday party. He really loved it.

Just as the family reacted differently when Lord Tavistock was desperately ill, so have they responded in different ways to his new approach to life. There has been a lot of readjustment.

'My son's recovery is really miraculous,' says the Duke of Bedford. 'It has been very gradual and incredibly slow, but for me who sees him a few times a year, the progress is always dramatic. His recovery is in the main due to his wife, his children, all the many people who helped him to walk, talk, read and write and the devotion of his wonderful friends. Now I see my dear son's body but it is inhabited by a different personality. Before he was a high-powered, ambitious, successful and tense man, whom I admired and respected. Today he is a much more relaxed and happy man. He smiles and laughs and enjoys each day as it comes. I love this man too and I hope he will have as much pleasure with his new personality as he had with his old one. Personally I feel he will. Despite my son's frustration at trying to find the right words to speak, I have now found him easier to talk to. He can now use one's help. My love and admiration for him are stronger than ever. His cheerful and open personality is a joy to see. I thank God and all those who made this possible from the bottom of my heart and in all humility.'

Jamie feels the change in his father is for the better. 'Before Daddy's stroke, I didn't see him that much, or have long conversations with him, because he was always very tired. He would burn himself out during the week in London and when I saw him at the weekend he would be exhausted or distracted. He was also much stricter and had quite a temper if he was provoked. He's much more relaxed now, he appreciates life, enjoys things more, is much less inhibited, says what he wants to say and does what he wants to do rather than what he thinks he should.

'For a few months after he came back to Woburn, he kept shouting at me to be quiet especially at mealtimes. I didn't get upset. I realised he wanted to assert himself and thought he would try it out on me. I know I talk too much anyway. I think he was frustrated that people weren't necessarily treating him with enough respect. I could take it and he doesn't do it any more. After me he tried asserting his authority on the dogs.

'Daddy and I now have a different relationship. Not only because I didn't know him well before, but because it is now much more natural and we are much closer. I think it's partly because once you've seen someone as helpless as Daddy was, when they've almost been at your mercy, you can't see them in the same way. You certainly can't think of them as the stern, fire-breathing dragon any more. I don't miss the discipline at all.'

Robbie, however, has mixed feelings about losing his father's discipline. 'I sometimes feel I have lost a very strong influence in my life. I now realise how much I relied on it being there and how much I used to bounce off it. I had and still do have a lot of respect for my father, but now I sometimes feel a little angry and sad that I've lost him as my guiding light. The person who used to discipline me and keep me in line is not there any more. There have been occasions during the last two years when things have happened that before his stroke, would have made him scream at me or give me a lecture. He doesn't now. I know it sounds strange, but every now and then I could do with a good lecture and although I hated them when I got them, I miss them now. It's not the same when my mother does it.

'I never had to discipline myself before because, like it or not, I knew he would track me down, either on the telephone or in person, and give me an earful which would bring me back. Now I have to look inside myself for those things. I never did anything really wrong. I just haven't been as quick at doing things as I should have been. I have no career, although I hope to develop one within the political aspects of the environment. I have always been interested in the environment, but since my father's illness I have concentrated on it much more. That is one positive aspect that has come out of his stroke.

'Generally I think that it was a very good thing that he had his stroke. He is himself now and not dealing with issues from his past like his mother having died early and not getting along with his father.

'I think he covered up a lot of emotions by working hard and now he's himself, he's able to enjoy life more. He's definitely easier to live with because he's more light-hearted and relaxed.'

Andrew remembers his father's strict discipline when he and Robbie were young. 'We didn't mess around with Daddy. If he said do something, we did it, but Daddy and I didn't really know each other. I respected him but there was a distance between us. He was always very disciplined in the home environment. I remember when I was about twelve, he decided that he would take Robbie and me away with him on our own for two weeks' holiday every alternate summer so that he would get to know us better. I was terrified at the thought, but in fact he was far more relaxed on holiday. I spent more time with Daddy than Robbie did because we both love shooting.

'When we were at home, however, we knew what we could and couldn't do. About twice a week he would beat us with a slipper on our bottoms, when he caught us doing something wrong. He was constantly making us write lines for things like not finishing our lunch or dinner, or if he caught us fighting, or our rooms were in a mess. We had to make sure our rooms were always tidy.

'The first time we really got to know each other was when I had my accident. He was very loving, understanding and caring when I was hospital. He was also very good when I was a student in America and got involved in business with a friend who had invented an anti-pollutant device for putting into cars. He invested some money in the company when it was just getting off the ground. It is now doing extremely well.

'The best thing to have come out of Daddy's stroke is that he is now much happier and more fun. He never showed his true feelings or let himself go before. All his cares and worries seem to have disappeared. You can laugh and joke and be more familiar with him. The stroke occurred just as he was achieving everything he thought he wanted, but perhaps he will now look back and realise that a lot of what he pushed himself to do or other people pressurised him into doing was unnecessary. Now he can climb off the business ladder and not care what other people think of him.

'He has the chance to concentrate on doing what he thinks is important. Perhaps he had to go through the first part of his life to appreciate the second.

'Socially too, he's much more open and relaxed, even at the most formal occasions. Some people can't cope with the change in him, they don't know what to talk to him about or if he can understand them. I don't think that matters.

'Daddy has now improved to such an extent that he has begun to see that there are a lot of things to consider as well as himself and has become more caring, which is very good for Mummy. There is still room for improvement. He has to understand that everyone can't continue to live their lives just for him. He's got to do more stimulating things, think for himself again, do things independently and by doing so learn to cope with reality. He is also very lax about physiotherapy and taking exercise. He doesn't seem to take on board the fact that if he gets too fat he might have a heart attack. His attitude is difficult for us to cope with, because we wouldn't want to go through another medical emergency with him.

'Although his stroke is obviously a terrible thing to have happened to him, it was marvellous for me to be able to help him recover. It's very nice for any child to have the opportunity to give something back to his parents.

'A son is constantly trying to live up to his parents' hopes and expectations. One always wants to prove to them that one can do things, but very rarely gets the opportunity. I was happy that I was needed and I felt there was no longer the distance between us that we used to have. Mummy and I were always convinced, however stupidly and wrongly it might have seemed at the time, that he would be himself again. We never looked on the black side, never thought he would die or be a vegetable.

'I would attribute his recovery first and foremost to Daddy himself, because I believe one has an element of control as to whether one lives or dies and Daddy was obviously determined to stay alive. There is without a doubt an "upstairs" element. There has been the incredible professional help of Alan Crockard, Eirian Jones and Tania Lorking and of course the warmth of family and friends.

'Because Daddy was such a private person, I think that if we had kept everyone away from him when he had his stroke, he might have felt very insecure about going out and seeing people again. Instead he feels he has nothing to hide. People know how bad he was and have been amazed at what an incredible recovery he has made. Everyone seems to care. When I went to the tailor, to a restaurant, or to the stables in Newmarket, everyone asked about him.

'As well as their genuine concern for Daddy, I'm also sure his stroke made them more aware of the frailty of life. If it can happen to someone who was only forty-eight and lived sensibly, it could happen to anyone. Equally, seeing him get better has given them a lot of hope. If Daddy can pull through, it is fantastic what doctors can do providing everyone helps each other.

'Since Daddy's stroke we've all got more involved in running Woburn, but I think there are too many people doing bits and pieces and it was a much smoother-running ship before when there was one boss. Apart from the Tina Turner concert last summer, I feel most things are in neutral. It's hard to plan because we don't know what is going to happen and we might all have to wait for another year or two until we do. Now Daddy is back on all levels, he and Mummy have got to do some serious thinking and talking about what they want to do in the future. Daddy's got to decide whether he wants to work on his stamina and throw himself back into Woburn so that everything is reported back to him again and Mummy's got to decide whether she wants to run it or not.

'Daddy's also got to find a simple way of updating his memory so that he doesn't have to rely entirely on other people who might at some point take advantage of him. At the moment he obviously needs to put much more energy into everything he does, and what he can do is governed by how tired he gets. I've had conversations with him since his stroke, where he has been just like he was before.

'He might find it slightly more difficult to get the words out and perhaps not say precisely what he means, but his ideas are still phenomenal. There are times when he really wants to concentrate and puts all his energy into something and then he is about 98 per cent of his pre-stroke self.

'But I think that takes up so much energy that he doesn't particularly enjoy it and I've noticed that if he doesn't want to do something, he pretends he can't. He's much more conscientious with the boards he sits on in the City. He knows he has responsibilities as a director and has to be on the ball, so he gets up early, reads the papers and makes sure he is clued up. With in-house meetings he takes a much more relaxed attitude.

'Invariably Daddy's progress has got slower, but we still have sudden breakthroughs or a conversation that makes us suddenly realise how much he's still improving.

'I know my parents feel anxious about giving me too much responsibility at Woburn, but it would be possible for me to run it and still work for Tattersalls in Newmarket. Woburn and Newmarket are only about an hour's drive apart and both places have their quiet times. The only problem is that it's difficult to feel relaxed at Woburn. You can't really let your hair down, get up late, not bother to shave and that sort of thing. You also tend always to be in the office.'

Lord Tavistock has, in fact, been involving himself at Woburn in a gentle way since he first came home in June 1988.

'The moment he came back he obviously wanted to look at his papers,' his secretary Cilla remembers. 'He is a director of Trafalgar House and started going to board meetings there from the beginning of 1989. In one way I felt he started doing things too quickly. But on the other hand, sitting in on meetings may well have added to the stimulation that has brought him to how he is today, which is incredible.

'When he first came back to Woburn, he'd sometimes come down in the morning and ask me to put his jumper on for him, because he couldn't work out which way round it went. He knew his head had to go through the large hole, but he couldn't work out what to do with the arms. I felt so embarrassed for myself and for him which I shouldn't have really. These days when he is feeling good, his decisions are just as they would have been before his stroke. What he would have said "no" to then, he says "no" to now. He just takes longer to arrive at his decision.'

Lord Tavistock now attends business meetings in London, speaks at dysphasic conferences and involves himself in the day-to-day running of the estate. His workload, however, is still carefully monitored. 'We try to limit his meetings to two a day because until now more than that has been too much for him,' says Cilla. 'Concentrating and talking to people are still tiring for him. Six months ago he found it too much of a distraction if he was talking to someone and another person interrupted. He used to become quite edgy, but he's much better now.

'I feel very responsible that if he is going to a meeting, he has everything he needs as far in advance as I can produce it for him so that he is totally genned up.'

Chuck Downer, because he only sees Robin at intervals, always notices his progress and is particularly aware of the changes in him. 'I think he's more adorable than ever. The damage caused by the stroke has erased a lot of his outer shell, and got rid of a lot of the emotional baggage he was carrying. Most of his childhood anger and sadness has disappeared and he wakes up friendly and happy. Other people can now see what I have always seen in him. Many people were afraid of him, but now he doesn't have to pretend to be someone he was not. In spite of this I still think his stroke was a tragedy and the cruellest thing to have happened to him. He's still very interested in what I'm doing, but we can't discuss the same serious matters we used to talk about. He can't remember the details of what went on before and it is very tiring for him to concentrate.'

Henrietta's friend Bunny Esterhazy recently asked Robin whether, if he had the choice, he would prefer to have had his stroke and be the man he is now, or not have had the stroke and continued as he was. 'He said he would definitely prefer to have had the stroke,' she says, 'because not only is he enjoying life more, but he is noticing things he never noticed. He looks out of the window and sees so much that is beautiful around him. In one way I'm almost happy for him because at last he is getting some fun out of life. He's even become slightly irresponsible. And because he is a more open person, even though he has difficulty in talking, he talks infinitely more now than he ever did.'

Henrietta is the person who knows more than anyone the nuances of the effect the stroke has had on her husband.

Robin's whole life has been geared to build and achieve. I'm the one who has had a privileged life. I've been able to do the things that interested me and develop outside interests. Robin, however, has been involved in business, in running the estate, and in the various background aspects to becoming a good duke. He has no hobbies, he doesn't read much, or take photographs, and never used to go to concerts, ballet or the opera. The only thing he really wanted to do was travel and he couldn't do that because he couldn't be away from Woburn for more than ten days at a time, otherwise things invariably go wrong. It used to upset me that we could never go away for more than ten days, but now Robin can, I feel I can't, nor do I want to.

His short-term memory is much better, but it isn't 100 per cent. I very often have to push the right button to help him. If I ask him, 'What did you do yesterday?' he might look at me and say, 'You know I can't answer that.' But if I ask, 'Did you go to Edinburgh yesterday?' he'll say, 'Of course I didn't go to Edinburgh. I went to there and there and there.' He has resigned from several directorships and when I told him how sad I was, he replied, 'You don't have to feel sorry for me, because after all I did succeed, didn't I?'

Luckily he is still only fifty-one, which is young enough to start again and now he doesn't have to do anything for the sake of achieving, just the things that interest him, which could be much more rewarding. It's up to him to decide what they are going to be. At the moment I still think his life needs to be stage-managed so he doesn't get hurt.

I feel his stroke was sent by God to say to him, 'For goodness' sake Robin, you've got the most wonderful life and you are wasting it.' Of course we would all say, 'If only he hadn't had it,' but that is the only 'if only'. Once he had suffered his stroke, everything down to the smallest detail has helped him recover as much as he has. Perhaps God even wanted him to feel grateful he had it. In fact Robin already is grateful, just as Andrew has been about his accident.

I think the stroke has been God-given to me too, in that Robin has now became a much more relaxed person. When I first got married I wouldn't have wanted someone so easy. It wouldn't have been good for me and I probably would have been impossible. But now Robin is bliss to live with and enjoys everything. Because very few people who have had a stroke as severe as Robin's, have ever made his sort of recovery, we are now in uncharted territory. When I consciously think about his future or discuss it with other people, I have a more restricted view of what it will be. However, my instinct tells me that there will be virtually nothing he won't be able to do if he wants to, and I wouldn't mind having a huge bet that time will prove my instinct is right.

Epilogue

by Lord Tavistock

Lord Tavistock has made such an amazing recovery that he is now able to look back on his life before his stroke and the illness itself with a degree of sensitivity and perspective that he would not have done before.

I can hardly remember anything between Christmas 1987 and August 1988 when I realised I was in the south of France. I cannot even remember totally the six months before my stroke, but I do remember feeling very unwell. I used to get a lot of headaches, but I never complained to anyone about them. I used to feel incredibly tired. My memory wasn't good. I became quite irritable. I felt something was wrong with me, but I didn't know what it could be. I didn't know what to do to relieve it. And I had such a lot of work to do.

I realised there was a lot of strain between Henrietta and myself. I wasn't sure why. I have only just worked out the reason for it. I was being very difficult at the time, largely because I was feeling unwell. My mind wasn't in the correct gear. We certainly weren't good together. We had a lot of difficulties both in the early years of our marriage and when we moved to Woburn. We were very close when we were at Chevington, however. That was a lovely time in our lives. I now feel that we are back close again, but in a different way. I know it sounds strange, but I think the stroke has done our marriage a lot of good.

Before the stroke I didn't realise I was ill. I just thought life was getting too much for me. But now I feel very happy about life. Despite the struggle to speak and write again, in a way it was a wonderful thing to happen. Otherwise, where was I going? I was beginning to feel my relationship with Henrietta might not have a future. I didn't

209

know what to do with my life. Now I feel lucky to be alive.

My last memory before the stroke was talking on the telephone to John de Havilland. Then I was in hospital. I can remember being very near to death. I didn't want to go and in a way I felt I had the ultimate decision. It is difficult to describe now what I felt then, but I was somewhere I had never been before. I knew I was almost but not quite dead. I was in a totally different world. It was very peaceful up there. I was sort of asked if I wanted to live. Although it wasn't that clear. It was rather like being in my own dream, except it couldn't have been, because I had no way of knowing what it was like up there. It will never all come back to me and I don't think it should. It lasted for a fleeting moment of time, but I don't know how long that time was and therefore it is difficult to re-create it again. After that somebody up there said, 'We don't think we want you yet.' It wasn't quite a voice, more a feeling. I don't know why they didn't want me and will always have that mystery in my mind. Someone up there must like me.

I can remember certain things in the hospital, usually negative ones. I remember barricading my room against the nurse, because I didn't like him. And I hated the physiotherapist sitting on my bed. I know that if I didn't like anyone, I wouldn't do anything for them. I can remember from the south of France onwards more clearly.

When I first realised I couldn't talk it was hell. I thought I was going mad. When I first started speech therapy with Eirian Jones, I felt that something was going to happen. At first I didn't realise that it wouldn't come back quickly. It took a while before I accepted that it would be ages before I could even put two words together. Eirian was always positive and always built upon whatever little I could do. She has helped me get dramatically better. Now my sentences aren't too bad. I know what words I want to use inside my head, but sometimes they won't come out. It used to make me cross and frustrated, but now I try to work round it. I try to see if I can put what I want to say another way when hopefully the right word will come out. Sometimes I use a synonym, other times I fall back on clichés. My writing is better and my spelling is improving although neither is there yet. I don't yet know how much more I shall improve. I accept that my memory will never be 100 per cent better. My aim is to get it back by 90 per cent. It's getting better, but it's not there yet. I'm trying to do things to help it improve and now always have a tape recorder with me, which is a tremendous help.

I think I have changed a lot since my stroke in both small and fundamental ways. I used to be very introverted and although I'm not an extrovert now, I am much more open. I was sometimes too formal, even a little pompous. I am more relaxed about my clothes. I don't feel the need to dress so formally. I used to smoke thirty cigarettes a day, now I don't. I now sleep well and have become less faddy about my food.

My attitude to work has changed enormously. I used to work very long hours. I had to prove myself. I wanted to do well and get to the top at an early age so I could feel proud of myself. I think I did in the end. I realise that I have done quite well with my career and my life. But my working hours were daft. I thought that that was all that life was about. My father hadn't done very well and I wanted to. He didn't find his feet until he opened Woburn to the public. After that I think he did incredibly well for twenty years. But it was a narrow life. He wasn't successful in worldly terms. I worked so hard I didn't even have holidays. I would now like a much more unstressful life. I wouldn't mind being more involved in Woburn again. I would also like to travel the world without having to rush back to work, which I never had time to do before.

I have hopefully also changed as a parent. I now admit that I was too strict with Andrew and Robbie. Because my mother died when I was five and I had two stepmothers, I didn't really know how to bring up children other than by being very strict. I was always trying to instil some discipline into them. Actually I don't think it has done them too much harm. I know my temper would sometimes go through the roof and I used to get incredibly cross with them. I haven't been so strict with Jamie. He's a wonderful child and very intuitive. He understands my problems and is very good with me. He often says to me, 'Don't worry, Daddy. If you can't say it, it doesn't matter.' He is of real help to me and it is very moving for me to have such a close relationship with him. I am very sorry that in my family things didn't always happen as happily as they should have done, but I'm not going to let it make me miserable. There is no point in that.

The children have told me that I wasn't a very good father, I have apologised to them and hopefully they will forgive me. I know I am a better father now and much more approachable.

I used to mind if people didn't like me. Now I genuinely don't. Some people have difficulties in speaking to me. I can see them thinking: Poor boy, he can't speak correctly. I realise some people treat me as a child, or talk down to me by speaking very slowly and using pidgin English. I tell myself that perhaps they are not worth communicating with and it also makes me more determined to get better as quickly as I can and show them. Other people haven't got a clue what to say to me, particularly, I'm afraid, my father. What many of them don't realise is that my comprehension is total.

Occasionally people try to pull the wool over my eyes, but I think they are now beginning to realise that there is little point in doing it. I don't care if people think I am thick because I can't always get the right words out. Other people are embarrassed by me or find coming to terms with the relaxed me very difficult. It doesn't hurt me at all. I am also much more honest. I realise I have changed a lot and the reason is that I feel incredibly lucky to be alive.

However, just to live isn't enough. I don't know yet what my life will be like in the future. I have the motivation to do something and even might have to tread on a few people's toes to do it, but I'll have to cope with that. The people at Woburn are very loyal to me. London, however, is different.

I would like the chance to get more involved in the estate, because it is time I did. I think Henrietta, Andrew, Robbie and Jamie are all a bit over-protective of me. But equally, I am very grateful to them for protecting me, because if they hadn't done so, I don't think I would have recovered so well. I hope they will soon let me do everything so that I can see what I am capable of doing.

Although intellectually I am ready to have an active working role, my memory and word-finding problems make it difficult for me. I also tire more easily.

I feel incredibly lucky to have been able to get over my stroke with the ability I now have to speak. I am trying to improve myself to the point where there is no improvement left to make and I'm not sure yet where that will be. I feel incredibly anxious about it all. The inside of me is fully aware of the state I am in, but I cope with it in a relaxed manner because that is the only way.

In the past I never used to take much notice of people with disabilities, but I have become much more sympathetic towards disabled people generally. We have donated funds to open a new six-bedroom surgical intensive care unit at the National Hospital, which is at the moment the most up to date in the world. I know that in the future a significant part of my life will be in helping other people whose language disability is greater than mine. Wherever I go on my travels I will try to see people who have had the same sort of speech problems as I have had. I want to persuade them that they shouldn't worry too much. They will get there, they should just be patient, put their thoughts together and take as long as they need to express themselves. They should work hard and hope to get back as much language as they can.

People who have difficulty in speaking often have very sad lives. Sometimes they lose their jobs. Often people are not willing or don't have enough time to sit down and talk to them. I want to explain to their families, to say, 'They will only get better if you talk to them, but you should also be patient and wait for their replies.' And I will say, 'Please don't hide them away.' I want people to see me as I am now and say that unless I had told them about my stroke, they would never have realised that I had been so ill. I want to give them hope that they or their loved one can do what I have done. I want to tell them that in the beginning I couldn't get two words together, but look and listen to me now. Improvements can take a long time, sometimes several years and people are not always willing to devote themselves to that.

Everyone was wonderful to me when I was so ill. I suppose that is how I have got better. Henrietta insisted that everyone around me was positive and there was someone with me round the clock. I was never alone. I know I was lucky. I only began to realise how much she has done for me about six months ago. I never thought anything about it before, but I now know how much she did behind the scenes. I have come to realise that I owe her a lot for my life. Without her and of course Andrew, Robbie, and Jamie and all the other people who helped, I don't know what would have happened to me.

I told Henrietta when we were teenagers that my ambition was to be a good duke. It still is. I have to maintain a certain dignity and behave accordingly. I want to try to help people lead a good life and to try to succeed myself. That is my destiny.

I am now no longer frightened of dying. I used to be, but never told anyone of my fear. To come back from what I had is amazing and I feel lucky to be alive. I am aware that something has happened in my head. There is a feeling that something has been taken out and that I have been put back together. It may sound strange but my head feels different. A little clearer, as if I have got rid of something that shouldn't have been there.

I don't regret what has happened to me. The stroke has made Henrietta and I reassess ourselves and find the worth in each other. I have never felt she has loved me as much as she does today.

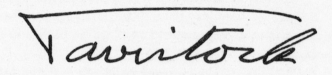